Kathy Schrock's
Every Day of the School Year Series

Daily Celebration Activities:
September through January

Midge Frazel

LINWORTH
LEARNING

A Publication of Linworth Learning

Linworth Publishing, Inc.
Worthington, Ohio

Published by Linworth Publishing, Inc.
480 East Wilson Bridge Road, Suite L
Worthington, Ohio 43085

ISBN 1-58683-070-8

5 4 3 2

❖ Table of Contents ❖

SEPTEMBER

OCTOBER

Table of Contents

NOVEMBER

DECEMBER

❖ Table of Contents ❖

JANUARY

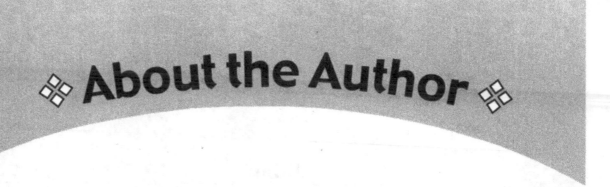

About the Author

*M*idge Frazel is a consultant specializing in educational technology. She designs and develops workshops for teachers to help them learn how to manage computer technology hardware and software productively and to integrate technology into the classroom curriculum. Readers can use Midge's Home Page <http://www.midgefrazel.net> as a classroom, library media center, or public library resource. She may be reached at *midgef@midgefrazel.net*. Midge has co-authored two books with Kathy Schrock and authored another available only in electronic format.

Midge celebrates National Blonde Day on July 9 and her favorite holiday falls on October 31.

Acknowledgements

I would like to thank the teachers who contributed their own classroom activities to celebrate. They are Kathy Wasik of Bridgewater, Massachusetts; Debbie Zakowski of Seekonk, Massachusetts; Gayle Bradbury of Somerset, Massachusetts; and last, my daughter, Heather Frazel, of Newton, Massachusetts. They gave freely of their precious time. These classroom-tested lessons are the heart of this book.

Thanks also to Kathy Schrock, whose encouragement and patience during this project kept me sane. Also, to my husband Steve for seeing nothing but my back at my computer for months! A special thank you to the librarians of the Bridgewater Public Library for their help with the print resources and to my co-workers for the technical help I needed as I went along.

There is so much in life to celebrate—at home, at school, at work, and in the world. I'd like to celebrate the lives of those who perished in the attack on America on September 11, 2001. Freedom is the ultimate celebration.

A Word From Kathy Schrock

elcome to the Every Day of the School Year Series! As an educator, library media specialist, and now technology administrator, I know how important it is for the classroom teacher to extend the learning experiences in the classroom. With the current focus on standards-based teaching, learning, and assessment, I felt it was important to supply classroom teachers and library media specialists with activities which directly support the curriculum, but, at the same time, allow for creative teachers to provide supplementary and extension activities for their students.

The activities in this series are varied in scope, but all of them provide practical tips, tricks, ideas, activities and units. Many of the activities include related print and Internet sites, which are easily collected by the classroom teacher before engaging in the activity. There are handouts, worksheets, and much more throughout the books, too. In my job as technology administrator for a school district, I am often able to plan lessons with teachers and visit classrooms to observe the teaching of the lesson. In addition, as the creator and maintainer, since 1995, of Kathy Schrock's Guide for Educators (http://discoveryschool.com/schrockguide/), a portal of categorized Web sites for teachers, I often receive e-mail from teachers who are searching for practical, creative, and easy-to-implement activities for the classroom. I hope this series provides just the impetus for you to stretch and enhance your textbook, lesson, and standards-based unit by use of these activities!

If you have any titles you would like to see added to the series, or would like to author yourself, drop me a note at kathy@kathyschrock.net

Kathy Schrock

⬧ How to Use this Book ⬧

The activities featured in this book give teachers the opportunity to start each day with a celebration, or to enrich their curriculum with an integrated celebration activity. Daily lessons can be enhanced by introducing interesting historical, cultural, literary and amusing events to spark students' interest in the world around them and to create excitement about a particular subject area. Melding the past with the present, and adding a splash of the future as a daily introductory event, can make a difference in the lives of your students.

For centuries, every nation, culture and society has set aside days for festivals, fiestas and thanksgiving. The celebrations presented here will help students understand and respect the varied customs and traditions that are the foundation of our American culture.

Art, music, physical education, science, history, literature, mathematics and geography all contain events to celebrate, and are each represented in this book. Many of the activities are interdisciplinary, which allow the integration of science, mathematics and the arts into language and social studies based lessons. This type of learning can connect many disciplines within the confines of a single school day and provide students with a basis for the deeper learning that happens in later grades.

The activities have been divided into monthly sections to fit easily into lesson plan preparations. As you plan, keep in mind the needs and ability levels of your students. Take notes on this year's experiences, considering your students level of interest, to help you plan for next year. This book contains fall/winter activities that start with the beginning of school in September and continues through the month of January. A companion book has celebration activities that cover February to June.

Journal writing is promoted as a central focus, to develop the critical thinking, organization and personal reflection skills essential for effective communication. Project-based work, both individual and teamed, is suggested as well as methods of effective presentation of the material learned. Rich with links to literature in print to promote success in reading, these activities also make connections to information found on the Internet to celebrate the best use of technology and print resources.

Tips for Using the Internet in the Classroom:

■ If you have a one-computer classroom, assign a team of students to work on the computer, using the prepared Web site resources as a guide. Each month, a new team can be "in charge."

■ If you have a computer lab available, pick celebrations that fit into the lab appointment schedule.

■ If you only have online access at one computer or have to use your personal home computer, mark those activities that fit your curriculum plan and concentrate on the technology integration at that point.

❖ How to Use this Book ❖

Following the theme of celebrations, the lessons in this book have strong ties to the national standards in language arts, social studies, and foreign languages. As you choose a daily event to celebrate, use the guidelines listed here to match the benchmarks of your individual state standards and frameworks.

In kindergarten through grade three, activities connect to the national standards in social studies revolving around the celebrations of home and community. By combining these ideals with the suggested readings and Web sites, and with the introduction of journal writing, these standards can be tied to NCTE standards one and five.

For students in grades four and five, continuing with the benchmarks established in the earlier grades, links can be made to the celebration of important dates in American history and the celebrations of other cultures. As students begin to conduct research, gather, evaluate and synthesize information, NCTE standard seven is met. Using technology as a process for effective communication ties to NCTE standard eight. Students will also be involved in NCTE standards eleven and twelve, which connect journal writing, reflection, and creative thinking to reading, writing and communication.

We all look forward to celebrations, and by using these lessons in the classroom, we can engage, motivate and inspire young learners.

Let's begin each school day with a celebration!

September

Activity 1:

Celebrate the First Day of School

Subject: Interdisciplinary

Grade level: 1 to 5

Welcome back to school! Traditionally, the first day of school has been set for the Wednesday after Labor Day, but many states and countries begin the school year in August or even have a year-round school calendar. Whenever this day falls for you, there's a good reason to celebrate the fresh-start feeling of a new beginning! If the smell of paper and a new box of crayons reminds you of your own primary school years, then you are ready to begin with these celebrations for your classroom.

Activity Title:
Classroom Celebrations

Materials:

Dictionaries (traditional print, CD-ROM, or Web-based), whiteboard or paper for recording brainstorming ideas, notebook journals for students, Reproducible Activity 1: Journal Cover, Reproducible Activity 1: Inside Cover: List of Holidays

Procedure:

Tell students that a special feature of the classroom year will be learning about celebrations. Challenge them to locate the definition of the word "celebration" or "celebrate" using the dictionary.

Gather the students for a whole-class brainstorming activity. Record student definitions on the whiteboard or on large paper. Ask students for reasons to celebrate (personal goals, sports achievements, birthdays, family and religious holidays) and record these ideas also.

Have the students decorate the cover of their journal (or use Reproducible Activity 1: Journal Cover) and record any special personal or family celebrations on the inside cover. Ask students to begin their journals with a personal learning goal to celebrate the first day of school and record it on the first page (or use Reproducible Activity 1: Inside Cover: List of Holidays).

Evaluation:

Students will be able to define the word "celebration," relate it to their own experience, and participate in a whole-class brainstorming activity as well as an individual reflective journal writing session.

Resources:

Merriam-Webster's Word Central
        <http://www.wordcentral.com>
Discovery School's Dictionary Plus
        <http://www.school.discovery.com/dictionaryplus/index.html>

Activity 1: Inside Cover: List of Holidays

Commonly Celebrated Holidays	**Date Celebrated**
New Year's Day	January 1
Inauguration Day	January 20 (every four years)
Martin L. King Day	Third Monday in January
Abraham Lincoln's Birthday	February 12
President's Day	Third Monday in February
George Washington's Birthday	February 22
Arbor Day	Last Friday in April
Mother's Day	Second Sunday in May
Memorial Day	Last Monday in May
Flag Day	June 14
Father's Day	Third Sunday in June
Independence Day	July 4
Labor Day	First Monday in September
Columbus Day	Second Monday in October
Veterans Day	November 11
Thanksgiving Day	Fourth Thursday in November
Christmas Day	December 25

Often Celebrated Holidays	**Date Celebrated**
Groundhog Day	February 2
St. Valentine's Day	February 14
April Fool's day	April 1
Halloween	October 31
St. Patrick's Day	March 17
Cinco de Mayo	May 5
Earth Day	April 22

Other Holidays

Chinese New Year
Passover
Easter
Yom Kippur
Chanukah
Kwanzaa

Enter Date Celebrated This Year

_____
_____
_____
_____
_____
_____
_____

Personal Holidays/Celebrations

Birthday

_____
_____
_____
_____

_____
_____
_____

Celebrate the Monarch Butterfly Migration

Subject: Science, Art, Language Arts
Grade level: K to 5

Participate in one of the miracles of natural science by learning about the migration of Monarch butterflies through an online project.

Activity Title:
Symbolic Butterfly Migration

Materials:

Web site access, paper butterfly outline (or Reproducible Activity 2: Monarch Butterfly Cutout), art materials, large mailing envelopes (2) with postage

Procedure:

Visit the Journey North Web site to obtain current information about the Symbolic Migration Project. Explain to the students how the Monarch butterflies migrate from North America to Mexico, Florida, and California to spend the winter.

Print out a Monarch butterfly outline (or Reproducible Activity 2: Monarch Butterfly Cutout) or draw your own and duplicate the pattern for each student.

Following the directions for participation, have the students decorate the paper butterflies and write a message for the students in Mexico (in Spanish if possible).

Follow the mailing directions to send the paper butterflies to Journey North. Be sure to mail them by the deadline given on the project page (about October 1).

Visit the Journey North Web site to see when United Parcel Service (UPS) picks up the paper butterflies to "migrate" them to Mexico. Track the package at the UPS Web site to simulate the actual migration.

Celebrate the migration again in the spring when butterflies return to your school.

Evaluation:

Students will learn to follow the migratory pattern of an insect by participating in an international project.

Resources:

Pringle, Laurence. *An Extraordinary Life: The Story of a Monarch Butterfly*. New York: Orchard Books, 1997.

Rosenblatt, Lynn M. *Monarch Magic! Butterfly Activities and Nature Discoveries*. Charlotte, VT: Williamson Publishing Co., 1998.

Journey North's Journey South Symbolic Migration <http://www.learner.org/jnorth/current.html>

Connecting Science and Literature: The Monarch Butterfly Project <http://www.midgefrazel.net/monarchtheme.html>

Activity 2: Monarch Butterfly Cutout

Name _____

Celebrate Mayflower Anniversary Day

Subject: Social Studies, Language Arts, Math
Grade level: 4 to 5

> On September 6, 1620, the Pilgrims and others set sail for the New World. Celebrate this day by fostering student's understanding of the hardships, bravery, and rewards of this exploration.

Activity Title:
Sailing to America on the Mayflower

Materials:

Supplies to create the time line, student journals, Web site access, materials listed for the Web activity Measure the Mayflower (if using), Reproducible Activity 3: Compare and Contrast Graphic Organizer

Procedure:

Read aloud excerpts from one of the historical fiction titles about the Mayflower crossing or visit Plimoth Plantation's Web site about the voyage.

Create a classroom time line from today's date back to the landing of the Mayflower in Plymouth Harbor on December 16, 1620. Use a cutout of the Mayflower to move the ship closer to Plymouth as a daily classroom activity.

Use a "Compare and Contrast" graphic organizer (Reproducible Activity 3: Compare and Contrast Graphic Organizer) to compare and contrast the voyage of the Mayflower with an expedition of a family to an unknown planet in the future. What hardships did the Pilgrims face that might be similar to those in space? Have the students reflect in their journals what it may have been like for them to leave their homes and travel to an unknown land to begin a new life.

For older students (grade 5 and up), use the Measure the Mayflower Web page activity to extend this lesson into math.

Evaluation:

Students will learn about the hazardous travel of the Mayflower in 1620 to prepare them for the lessons of the celebration of Thanksgiving. Students will learn more about the history of journal keeping for preparation in using primary sources in the classroom.

Resources:

Lasky, Kathryn. *A Journey to the New World: The Diary of Remember Patience Whipple: Mayflower/Plimoth Colony 1620*. New York: Scholastic, 1995.

Rinaldi, Anne. *The Journal of Jasper Jonathan Pierce: A Pilgrim Boy, Plimoth Plantation, 1620*. New York: Scholastic, 2000.

The Mayflower Voyage
<http://www.plimoth.org/Library/voyage.htm>

The Mayflower Story: Measure the Mayflower Activity
<http://www.elm.maine.edu/assessments/Mayflower/measure.stm>

Activity 3: Compare and Contrast Graphic Organizer

Name _____

Compare	Contrast

Name _____

Compare	Contrast

Celebrate National Grandparent's Day

Subject: Interdisciplinary

Grade level: K to 5

The idea of celebrating Grandparent's Day started with Marian McQuade to foster awareness of loneliness of elderly men and women in nursing homes. It is a national holiday, proclaimed by Presidential Proclamation, and is celebrated on the first Sunday following Labor Day.

Activity Title:

Importance of Multigenerational Family Life

Materials:

Student reflective journals, art supplies for display, Web site access

Procedure:

Create a portable, bulletin board-sized display of student-generated artwork with brightly colored drawings of fall topics to be delivered to a local nursing home to be placed in their community room.

In the students' reflective journals, have them describe their grandparents and tell a story about something they enjoy doing with a grandparent. Older students can create a short family tree by interviewing their parents and grandparents.

Read the story *Zero Grandparents* or *Hooray for Grandparents* (Grades 1-2) to introduce to the class how it feels to be a student who has no grandparents to participate in Grandparent's Day at school.

Evaluation:

Students will gain insight into the importance of learning about generations in families and how families spend time together to learn about past events in the lives of family members.

Resources:

Edwards, Michelle. *Zero Grandparents*. San Diego: Harcourt Brace, 2001.
Carlson, Nancy. *Hooray for Grandparent's Day*. New York: Viking, 2000.
Grandparent's Unit
     <http://www.teacherfeatures.com/units/grandpar.html>

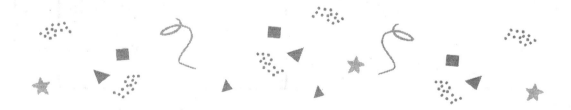

Celebrate National 5-A-Day Week

Subject: Health, Science
Grade level: K to 5

National 5-A-Day is celebrated during the second full week of September to promote the eating of five or more servings of fruits and vegetables for improved health. Started in 1991, this celebration began with the collaboration between the National Cancer Institute and the Produce for Better Health Foundation.

Activity Title:
Healthy Eating for Life

Materials:

Web site access, art materials, newspaper or magazine ads with pictures and prices of fruits and vegetables

Procedure:

Visit the Web site and order the free CD-ROM using school letterhead. Schools can order enough for each teacher's classroom or computer lab free of charge.

At the Web site, print the 5-A-Day Activity sheets for students. The Web site also contains a lesson for each day of 5-A-Day Week.

Create a classroom collage of fruits and vegetables. Which fruits and vegetables are the most or least expensive? What is the favorite fruit of the class?

Evaluation:

Students will gain an understanding of better nutrition to begin a lifetime of good eating habits.

Resources:

Eat 5 A Day
    <http://www.5aday.com>

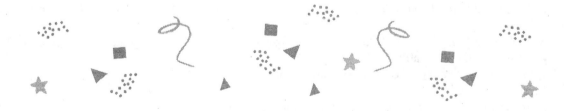

Celebrate Chocolate Day

Subject: Interdisciplinary
Grade level: K to 5

Celebrate the life's work of Milton S. Hershey on his birthday! Milton S. Hershey (1857–1945) is called the "Chocolate King" because he is famous for his chocolate confections and also because of the community he built in Pennsylvania, which exists to this day. He kept his employees and their families working during the Great Depression of the 1930s and provided chocolate bars for soldiers fighting in World War II. Known for his philanthropic nature, Hershey was devoted to children, building schools, and orphanages. His most famous candy is the Hershey's Chocolate Bar.

Activity Title:
How Is Chocolate Made?

Materials:

Web site access, encyclopedias (traditional print, CD-ROM, or Web-based), suggested readings on Milton S. Hershey, chocolate kisses (optional)

Procedure:

Use an encyclopedia to research the history of chocolate. Have the students visit the Hershey Web site to find out what chocolate is and how it is manufactured.

Have the students read about Milton Hershey's life and discuss the importance of community. Have the students define "philanthropy."

Evaluation:

Student will research the history and manufacture of chocolate and learn about the philanthropic life of Milton S. Hershey.

Resources:

Burford, Betty. *Chocolate by Hershey: A Story About Milton S. Hershey*. Minneapolis: Carolrhoda Books, Inc., 1994.
Simon, Charnan. *Milton Hershey: Chocolate King, Town Builder*. New York: Children's Press, 1998.
Hershey's Virtual Tour (printable)
    <http://www.hersheys.com/tour/printversion.html>
Hershey's History of Chocolate
    <http://www.hersheys.com/consumer/history/index.html>
Milton S. Hershey
    <http://www.hersheys.com/about/milton/index.html>

Celebrate Potato Day Festival

Subject: Language Arts
Grade level: K to 1

> Harvesting vegetables to prepare for the long winter ahead is a special event in the fall. Celebrate the Potato Day Festival (September 14 to 16) with this literature-based lesson.

Activity Title:

The Enormous Potato Lesson by Debbie Zakowski
Kindergarten Teacher, Central Falls (Rhode Island) School District

Materials:

Suggested readings, sentence strips, whiteboard, materials for class book, Web site access

Procedure:

Before Reading the Folktales

Ask the class to look at the cover of the book and predict what the story will be about. As the students suggest possible story ideas, list them on a chalk or whiteboard. After all ideas have been solicited, ask them to "read" the list with you. (Read the word first and encourage the group to repeat the word.) When finished, let them know that they are "wonderful readers."

Read the title of the book and determine if there is a match to one of their suggestions.

Ask the students the definition of "enormous." Show a visual representation of enormous by showing the size with your hands and arms.

Ask students to tell you what letter begins the word "potato."

Reading the Folktales: Venn Diagram Activity (two class days)

Read *The Enormous Potato*. Have students volunteer "Things we noticed in the book" and write each on a sentence strip.

Read *The Enormous Turnip* and repeat the previous steps. Using a Venn diagram previously created on the whiteboard, place the strips on the diagram. In the center section, review "What is the same?"

Additional Activities

Role-play the story with one student who is the potato (child sits in a chair holding on tightly to the seat) and others who are the farmer, wife, daughter, dog, cat, and mouse. Students will learn that it is not the work of one, but of all pulling together that releases the potato from the soil.

Each student will contribute a page to a class book (What Is Enormous?) using the sentence frame: (child's name)'s Enormous _____. Remind the students that whatever food they choose, it must be enormous.

Evaluation:

Students will learn to compare and contrast two folktales using a Venn diagram, learn the word "enormous," and understand the benefits of teamwork.

Resources:

Davis, Aubrey. *The Enormous Potato*. Buffalo, NY: Kids Can Press, Ltd., 1997.
Parkinson, Kathy. *The Enormous Turnip*. Niles, IL: Albert Whitman and Co., 1986.
The Enormous Potato Web Lesson
    <http://www.ri.net/schools/Central_Falls/ch/heazak/enorpota.html>

Celebrate Substitute Teacher Appreciation Week

Subject: Art, Language Arts

Grade level: K to 5

> Preparing students for those days when the classroom teacher is absent from the classroom is important to the community nature of the elementary school years. Setting up classroom rules of conduct and how to work with others is essential for the first month of school.

Activity Title:

Appreciate the Substitute Teacher

Materials:

Art supplies for making paper greeting cards, Web site access for electronic greeting cards, a list of the teachers who are on the substitute calling list obtained from the office staff

Procedure:

Use dictionary skills to define the words "substitute" and "appreciation." Explain the classroom rules for working with a substitute teacher. Brainstorm where some special activities might fit into the classroom day.

Create greeting cards (paper or electronic) to distribute to these individuals or create a bulletin board display in the school hallway or lunchroom.

Evaluation:

Students will learn what will happen in their classroom if the classroom teacher is absent and learn something about (or meet) the teachers who work as substitutes.

Resources:

Blue Mountain Electronic Greeting Cards
    <http://www.bluemountain.com>

Celebrate Citizenship or Constitution Day

Subject: Social Studies

Grade level: 4 to 5

On September 17, 1787, the Constitutional Convention in Philadelphia voted unanimously to approve the Constitution of the United States. Each year Americans celebrate this day of freedom by learning about the Constitution. Immigrants to this country may choose this day to become citizens of the United States.

Activity Title:
The Blessings of Liberty

Materials:

Web site access

Procedure:

Write the Preamble to the Constitution on the whiteboard as a celebration of We the People. Use dictionary skills to define the word liberty. Have students recite the words together.

Students in the past were required to recite and memorize as a regular part of the school day. Brainstorm with the students what is meaningful about recitation and what is not.

Evaluation:

Students will begin to learn about the Constitution of the United States by using materials available from the National Archives and Record Administration.

Resources:

Constitution Day at NARA
   <http://www.nara.gov/teaching/constitution/home.html>
Constitution Day
   <http://www.constitutionday.com>

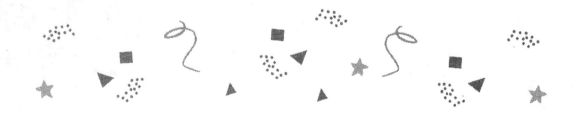

Celebrate International Day of Peace

Subject: Interdisciplinary

Grade level: K to 5

The United Nations General Assembly opens its sessions for the year on the International Day of Peace. Proclaimed in 1981, this day in September marks the desire of the world's people for peace. It begins with a special ringing of the Peace Bell.

Activity Title:
Peaceful Days

Materials:

Dictionaries or encyclopedias (traditional print, CD-ROM, or Web-based), a copy of the school district policy on conflict resolution or bullying, student journals

Procedure:

Use dictionary skills to define "peace." Brainstorm the word "peace" as it applies to the classroom and to the school. Emphasize peaceful play in the schoolyard at all times.

Older students may understand conflict resolution by learning about present and past peaceful leaders.

Evaluation:

Students will be able to define peace and describe its meaning in their lives. They will understand the school policy on resolving conflicts and how to get help in a conflict situation.

Resources:

The United Nations CyberSchoolbus
     <http://www0.un.org/cyberschoolbus/index.html>

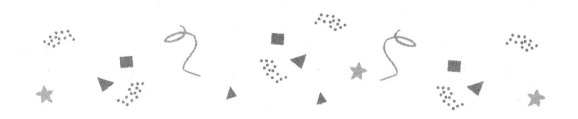

Celebrate National Literacy Month

Subject: Reading, Language Arts

Grade level: K to 5

Celebrate National Literacy Month by scheduling a visit to the school library media center or the children's room of the local public library.

Activity Title:
Everybody Read!

Materials:
None

Procedure:

Ask your students if any of them participated in a summer reading program. Ask them to tell about their favorite book.

Schedule a visit to the school library media center or the children's room of the local public library. Consult with your school library media staff or a children's librarian to find out what resources are available for your class.

Start a schedule of independent reading time in your classroom week.

Evaluation:

Students will begin a lifelong love of reading for themselves and family members.

Resources:

This is a good time to look through this book and see what library books you will need to use for future celebrations and how you can reserve them for use in the classroom.

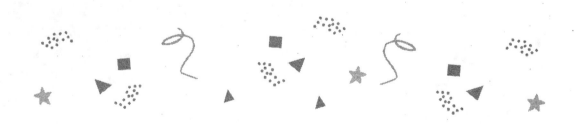

Celebrate the First Day of Fall

Subject: Science

Grade level: K to 5

> The experience of the changing of the seasons varies greatly from location to location. Help students celebrate fall by learning the essentials about the cycle of photosynthesis.

Activity Title:
Fall Changes in the Air

Materials:
Web site access, books on the topic

Procedure:

All leaves contain chlorophyll, which is a green pigment with the capability to capture light energy and convert that energy into sugar. This process is called photosynthesis. In the fall, the daylight gets shorter and there is not enough light or water for photosynthesis. The green chlorophyll disappears and the other pigments (yellow, orange, red and purple) that have been there all along show up because the chlorophyll does not cover them up anymore. Use books or the Web site to explain this process to the students.

If you have fall foliage in your area, gather leaves to make outlines of the shapes of the leaves. Prepare a collage to hang in the classroom.

Use an almanac to list the times for sunrise and sunset for the next month showing how much daylight is lost between the first and last days of the month. Find out why daylight savings time is observed.

Evaluation:

Students will learn about photosynthesis, relating it to the change in the color of the leaves in the fall. Students may learn about daylight savings time in this activity.

Resources:

Why Do Leaves Change Color in the Fall?
    <http://www.sciencemadesimple.com/leaves.html>
BrainPOP: Autumn Leaves
    <http://www.brainpop.com/science/ecology/autumnleaves>

Celebrate Ice Cream Cone Day

Subject: Math

Grade level: K to 5

> Celebrate the birthday of the ice cream cone! Italo Marchoiny, an Italian immigrant, was selling lemon ice from a pushcart in New York when he decided to create a paper cone (later it was pastry) to hold the ice. The patent for this "ice cream cone mold" was applied for on September 22, 1903, but not issued until December of that year.

Activity Title:
Favorite Flavors

Materials:

Computer spreadsheet graphing software or paper graphs

Procedure:

Ask the school parent organization to assist with the ice cream cone social event.

Create a class survey of favorite flavors of ice cream and prepare a classroom chart of the most favorite and least favorite flavors. Older students may use a spreadsheet for this activity and create different kinds of graphs.

Create a survey chart for students to ask another class for their favorite flavors. Compare those results to the results of their classmates.

Students can also price ice cream in the local grocery store and report the most expensive and least expensive brands by weight and cost per gallon.

Evaluation:

Students will learn to make a simple graph of the favorite flavors of ice cream of the class, prepare a survey of students in another class, and enjoy ice cream cones as a treat. This celebration could be a whole school event!

Resources:

Ben and Jerry
    <http://www.benjerry.com>
Make Ice Cream.com
    <http://www.makeicecream.com>

Celebrate Pioneer Days

Subject: Social Studies, Language Arts

Grade level: 3 to 5

Celebrate Pioneer Days with readings from the pioneer life of Laura Ingalls Wilder. This activity can be related to a larger unit on the Westward Movement or migration.

Activity Title:

Harvest

Materials:

Suggested reading, Web site access

Procedure:

Read Chapter 11, "Harvest," in *Little House in the Big Woods*, aloud to the class.

Ask the students to compare the "work" of harvest with the tasks performed in the fall months today. Find out how wheat is harvested. Discuss "crying wolf" as a method of getting attention. Discuss bee stings and how they are treated.

Visit the Web site to learn more about the pioneer days.

Evaluation:

Students will experience the "pioneer spirit" with a seasonal story.

Resources:

Wilder, Laura Ingalls. *Little House in the Big Woods*. New York: Harper and Bros., 1932.
42Explore: Pioneer Life
    <http://educapes.com/42explore/pioneer.htm>

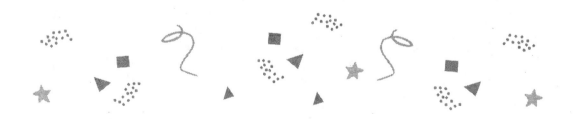

Celebrate National Honey Month

Subject: Science

Grade level: 1 to 5

Celebrate the sticky life of the honeybee during National Honey Month.

Activity Title:

Busy as a Bee

Materials:

Web site access, visit from a local beekeeper, honey for tasting

Procedure:

Invite a local beekeeper to visit to teach more about honey. Have honey available for tasting. Prepare for the classroom visit by reading about bees and honey production.

Evaluation:

Students will gain understanding of the life cycle of the honeybee and the industry of beekeeping and honey production.

Resources:

The Story of Honey
   <http://www.nhb.org/download/storyofhoneyweb.pdf>
The Honey Files: A Bees Life (with Teacher's Guide)
   <http://www.honey.com/kids/video/index.html>

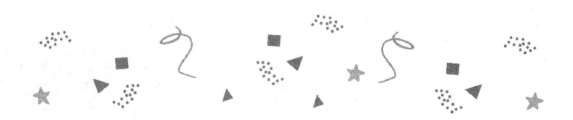

Celebrate Johnny Appleseed Day

Subject: Social Studies, Language Arts, Science

Grade level: K to 2

John Chapman dedicated his life to the planting of apple seedlings all over the American West. He had an uncanny knack for finding just the right spot to plant trees that would survive to this day. Celebrate apples on his birthday, September 27.

Activity Title:

An Apple a Day

Materials:

Apples, suggested reading, lemon juice

Procedure:

Have students read about Johnny Appleseed and write a paragraph about this American legend. Older students may write about apple trees in their journals.

Eat apples or applesauce, or drink apple juice to provide healthy eating. As a science activity, have students observe what happens when cut apple slices are exposed to the air. What happens to cut slices that have been dipped in lemon juice?

Evaluation:

Students will learn about the life of a man whose dedication to his work and simple lifestyle created a legend of an American hero. Students will continue to learn about healthy eating habits.

Resources:

Kellogg, Steven. *Johnny Appleseed: A Tall Tale*. New York: William Morrow and Co., 1998.
The Johnny Appleseed Home Page
    <http://www.msc.cornell.edu/~weeds/SchoolPages/Appleseed/history.html>
42Explore Topic: Apples
    <http://eduscapes.com/42explore/apples.htm>

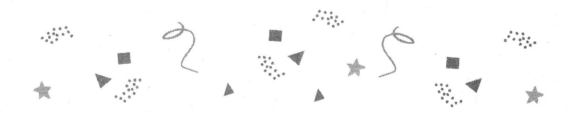

Activity 17:

Celebrate Kiwanis Kids Day

Subject: Interdisciplinary
Grade level: K to 5

Kiwanis International celebrates Kiwanis Kids Day on the fourth Saturday in September.

Activity Title:
Kids in the Community

Materials:

Contact a local chapter of Kiwanis International to see what activities for your students are available.

Procedure:

Send home information about a local celebration happening on the fourth Saturday of September with materials from a local chapter of Kiwanis International.

Evaluation:

Students will connect celebrations in the classroom and home to those in the community. Students will begin understanding the concept of fundraising for youth.

Resources:

Kiwanis International
    <http://www.kiwanis.org>

Activity 18:

Celebrate Frisbee Day

Subject: Physical Education

Grade level: K to 5

Believe it or not, the Frisbee was popularized by college students throwing the pie plates of the Frisbie Pie Company. An engineer named Fred Morrison brought the idea to Wham-O toy company, originally calling the item the "Pluto Platter." Executives at Wham-O Toys later renamed the toy the Frisbee, after its humble beginnings.

Activity Title:
Invention of the Frisbee

Materials:
Ask the Physical Education department of your school district to assist you and your school physical education teacher with this special event. Have enough Frisbees for each member of the class.

Procedure:
Invite the physical education teacher to the Invention of the Frisbee Day celebration. Practice Frisbee throwing in the schoolyard. Older students can play a game of ultimate Frisbee.

Evaluation:
Students will learn about the invention of the Frisbee, practice using one, and understand how a simple toy can become a sport.

Resources:
Hoffman, David. *Kid Stuff: Great Toys from Our Childhood*. San Francisco: Chronicle Books, 1996.
Invention of the Frisbee
    <http://www.ideafinder.com/history/inventions/story008.htm>
Newton's Apple: Frisbee Physics
    <http://www.pbs.org/ktca/newtons/9/frisbee.html>

Activity 19:

Celebrate Babe Ruth's Famous Day

Subject: Physical Education, Language Arts

Grade level: 3 to 5

On October 1, 1932, Babe Ruth played an amazing game of baseball. Celebrate the life of this warm and generous man by learning about past baseball heroes.

Activity Title:
Home Run!

Materials:

Web site access, suggested reading, student journals

Procedure:

Sports legends are larger-than-life heroes for students. Use the suggested reading to tell the story of the great Babe Ruth (1895–1948).

Have students use the American Memory Web site on Baseball Cards of the early years of baseball to learn about the past of this American sport. Have students design a baseball card in their journal.

Evaluation:

Students will learn about real-life sport figures and how they became legends.

Resources:

Burleigh, Robert. *Home Run*. New York: Harcourt Brace and Co., 1998.
National Baseball Hall of Fame: Babe Ruth
    <http://baseballhalloffame.org/hofers_and_honorees/hofer_bios/ruth_babe.htm>
American Memory: Baseball Cards 1887-1914
    <http://memory.loc.gov/ammem/bbhtml/bbhome.html>

Celebrate Leif Erikson Day

Subject: Social Studies, Language Arts
Grade level: 4 to 5

On October 9, celebrate the discovery of North America in the year 1000 by the Norse explorer Leif Erikson.

Activity Title:
Rune Writing

Materials:

Web site access, suggested reading, globe

Procedure:

Talk about who discovered America. Use the globe to have students locate the Scandinavian countries where the Vikings used to live.

Use the suggested Web sites to learn about Leif Erikson and to learn about the Rune writing.

Evaluation:

Students will learn about Leif Erikson and other Vikings, and explore a Rune writing activity.

Resources:

Jensen, Malcolm C. *Leif Erikson: The Lucky*. New York: Franklin Watts, 1979.
Leif Erikson
    <http://www.mnc.net/norway/LeifErikson.htm>
Dr. Annette Lamb's Viking Theme Page
    <http://eduscapes.com/42explore/viking.htm>
Rune Writing
    <http://www.pbs.org/wgbh/nova/vikings/runes.html>

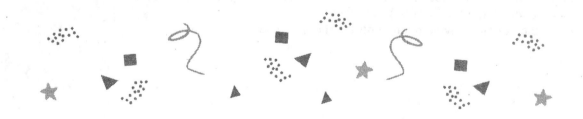

Celebrate Learning About Bats

Subject: Science, Reading, Language Arts
Grade level: 2 to 3

Are you nearly bats? If the answer is "Yes!" then fall is the time to celebrate learning about bats. For many classrooms, this can be a beginning of thematic learning and a month-long event. If your school doesn't celebrate Halloween, plan some of this activity for that day.

Activity Title:
Going Bats

Materials:

Stellaluna by Janell Cannon, Web site access, Reproducible Activity 21: KWL Graphic Organizer

Procedure:

Begin a seasonal science unit by using the KWL model (Reproducible Activity 21: KWL Graphic Organizer) to help your students brainstorm about bats. Read *Stellaluna* to the class. Use the Web to find out more about bats.

Evaluation:

Students will see the connection between science and literature by reading about bats.

Resources:

Cannon, Janell. *Stellaluna*. San Diego: Harcourt, Inc., 1993.
Gander Academy's Bats Theme Page
     <http://www.stemnet.nf.ca/CITE/bats.htm>
Bats4Kids: Bats, Bats, Everywhere
     <http://members.aol.com/bats4kids/index.htm>

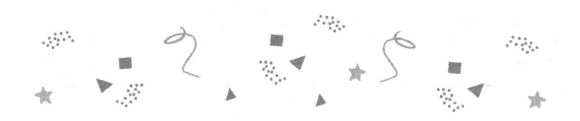

Activity 21: KWL Graphic Organizer

Name _____

Know	Want to Know	Learned

Name _____

Know	Want to Know	Learned

Activity 22:
Celebrate Columbus Day

Subject: Interdisciplinary
Grade level: K to 5

Celebrate the explorations of Christopher Columbus. Columbus was sure of himself, and his determination and positive attitude were the valuable traits that made him famous.

Activity Title:
Discover America

Materials:
Suggested reading, Web site access, student journals

Procedure:
The story of the voyage of Columbus and his ships is familiar to most students. Extend this knowledge by discussing the journal writing of the sea: the ship's log. Have the students write an imaginary ship log entry in their journal.

Use the Web sites to read parts of Columbus' journal. Was he trying to impress the readers with his ideas and accomplishments?

Evaluation:
Students will learn explorers did not always know where they were going, didn't know what to do when they arrived, and learned many lessons from making mistakes.

Resources:
Fritz, Jean. *Where Do You Think You're Going Christopher Columbus?* New York: Putnam, 1980.
Excerpts from the Journal of Columbus
   <http://www.fordham.edu/halsall/source/columbus1.html>
A Christopher Columbus Time line
   <http://www1.minn.net/~keithp/cctl.htm>
Kids Domain: Christopher Columbus Resource List
   <http://www.kidsdomain.com/holiday/columbusday.html>

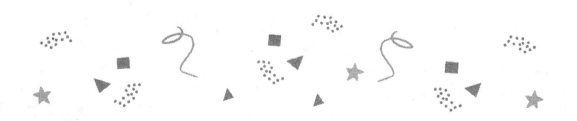

Celebrate Computer Learning Month

Subject: Technology Integration
Grade level: K to 5

> The Computer Learning Foundation's goal is to improve the quality of education and to prepare students for the workplace through the use of technology.

Activity Title:
Why WebQuests?

Materials:

Web site access

Procedure:

Bernie Dodge and Tom March invented WebQuests as a way to teach critical thinking via the Web. These online projects follow their model but are designed by classroom teachers for students to use. As with all Web pages, teachers should match the WebQuest to a specific curriculum goal and evaluate the contents prior to using it with students.

Explore the WebQuest Matrix of examples, find one for your class and use it during Computer Learning Month in the classroom or lab.

Evaluation:

Students will learn about online projects by completing a WebQuest.

Resources:

Computer Learning Month
     <http://www.computerlearning.org>
The WebQuest Page
     <http://edweb.sdsu.edu/webquest/webquest.html>

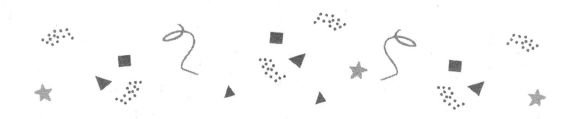

Celebrate Pledge Across America Day

Subject: Social Studies

Grade level: 2 to 5

Celebrate the Pledge of Allegiance on October 12 as a whole-class activity. All across America, schools will be holding a synchronized recitation of this pledge to honor Benjamin Harrison, for which the pledge was written in 1892.

Activity Title:
With Liberty and Justice for All

Materials:

Encyclopedias and dictionaries (traditional print, CD-ROM, or Web-based)

Procedure:

Ask the students to write the Pledge of Allegiance in their journals. "I pledge allegiance to the flag of the United States of America and to the republic for which it stands: one nation under God, indivisible, with liberty and justice for all." (Francis Bellamy, 1892)

Ask students to use dictionary skills to look up the words "pledge," "allegiance," and "indivisible."

Evaluation:

Students will learn more about the Pledge of Allegiance.

Resources:

Kallen, Stuart A. *The Pledge of Allegiance*. Minneapolis: Abdo & Daughters, 1994.
Morgan, H. Wayne. Discovery Channel School: World Book Online: "Benjamin Harrison." 26 July 2001
    <http://www.discoveryschool.com/homeworkhelp/worldbook/atozhistory/h/247260.html>

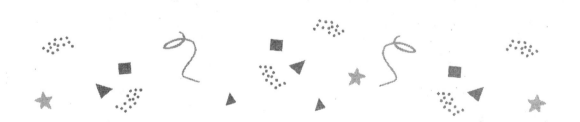

Celebrate Mystery Series Week

Subject: Reading

Grade level: 4 to 5

Everyone loves a good mystery! They are popular with adults and children alike, and figuring out "who, what, when, where, and why" is the best critical thinking tool. Celebrate the first full week of October by introducing a book in a mystery series.

Activity Title:
It's a Mystery!

Materials:

Web site access, juvenile mystery series books

Procedure:

Studying the mystery genre is a great fall and winter free time reading activity. Books in a mystery series, like the Nancy Drew books, can teach students the sequential nature of character development in an exciting way.

Students will write their own mini-mystery that includes all the classic elements of the mystery story.

Evaluation:

Students will develop essential critical thinking skills by reading mysteries in print and online.

Resources:

Learning with Mysteries: Why Mysteries? (for teachers)
    <http://www.mysterynet.com/learn/>
Mystery Net's Kids Mysteries
    <http://kids.mysertynet.com>
Mystery Book Report Form
    <http://www.abcteach.com/bookreports/mystery.htm>
Challenging Students with Mystery Stories
    <http://www.yale.edu/ynhti/curriculum/units/1989/4/89.04.06.x.html>

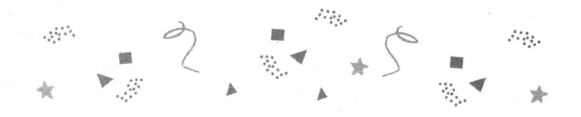

Celebrate Dictionary Day

Subject: Language Arts

Grade level: 3 to 5

Dictionary Day celebrates the Birthday of Noah Webster, who was born on October 16, 1758.

Activity Title:
Word To the Wise

Materials:

Dictionary (traditional print, CD-ROM, or Web-based), Web site access, student journals

Procedure:

Students will learn how the dictionary was created by learning about Noah Webster. If you have Web access, check the Cool Words Archive. Visit the school library to find out how many different types of dictionaries are available.

Evaluation:

Students will improve their dictionary skills.

Resources:

Ferris, Jeri. *What Do You Mean? A Story about Noah Webster*. Minneapolis: Carolrhoda, Inc., 1988.
Inkwell to Internet: From Noah Webster
    <http://www.m-w.com/about/noah.htm>
Noah Webster's House Museum
    <http://www.ctstateu.edu/noahweb/index.html>
Cool Words Archive (by month)
    <http://www.m-w.com/lighter/cool/coolarc.htm>

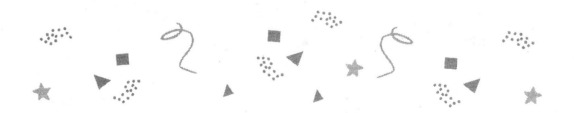

Celebrate School Librarian Day

Subject: Interdisciplinary

Grade level: 5

> Celebrate this day with a visit to the school library or media center. Interview a librarian to learn more about this important information specialist in your school.

Activity Title:
Information Specialists

Materials:

Clipboard with paper, pencils, whiteboard, tape recorder (or AlphaSmart)

Procedure:

Brainstorm with your students some questions to ask the school librarian. Some of these questions should relate to the type of education this person has received, which may be different from the classroom teacher.

Have the students write the questions in their journals. They may need to tape record the answers for their report. How does the job of this person differ from the job of a public librarian?

Evaluation:

Students will improve their interview skills by preparing questions, asking questions, and assembling the information gathered into their writing.

Resources:

Transcribing an Interview
   <http://hewit.unco.edu/sosc3006/students/culp/PROJECTS/Project5/lessons/Lesson%20plan.htm>

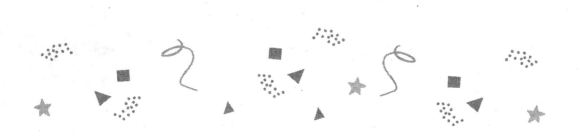

Celebrate Invention of the Light Bulb Day

Subject: Science

Grade level: 2 to 4

> Celebrate inventors with Thomas Alva Edison's October 19, 1879 invention of the incandescent light bulb.

Activity Title:
Inventing the Light Bulb

Materials:
Clear light bulb, dictionaries (traditional print, CD-ROM, or Web-based)

Procedure:
Have the students use dictionary skills to look up the word "incandescent" and write it in their journals.

Purchase a clear light bulb for the students to examine. Emphasize safe handling of glass and electricity.

Evaluation:
Students will learn about inventors and learn about safe use of electricity.

Resources:
Invention of the Light Bulb
<http://www.enchantedlearning.com/inventors/edison/lightbulb.shtml>
Lewis H. Latimer
<http://web.mit.edu/invent/www/inventorsI-Q/latimer.html>

Activity 29:
Celebrate Drawing Day

Subject: Art

Grade level: 3 to 4

> Celebrate Ed Emberley's birthday on October 19 by experimenting with drawing ideas from one of his books.

Activity Title:
Thumbprint Art

Materials:

Stamp pad, drawing paper, pen

Procedure:

Ed Emberley is well known for his simple-to-do drawings made from stamped images of thumbprints. Students can create sequenced drawings by following the steps to add to their own thumbprint. For this activity, have students create the bee, caterpillar, pumpkin, or frog to use as decoration for their journals or for illustrations in creative writing stories.

Evaluation:

Students will experiment with learning simple drawing.

Resources:

Emberley, Ed. *Ed Emberley's Great Thumbprint Drawing Book*. Boston: Little, Brown and Co., 1977.
Ed Emberley's Biography
    <http://teacher.scholastic.com/authorsandbooks/authors/emberley/bio.htm>

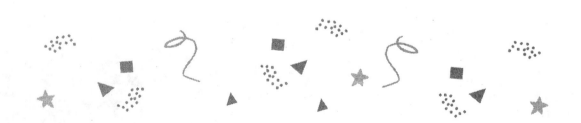

Activity 30:

Celebrate International Whale Watching Day

Subject: Science, Language Arts

Grade level: 2 to 4

> Even if you don't live near the ocean, you can still participate in a whale-watching event via the Web. Celebrate October 21 by learning more about whales.

Activity Title:
Whale of an Experience

Materials:
Whale-watching field trip, books on whales, Web site access

Procedure:
If possible, plan a whale-watching field trip (you may have to do this at the beginning of the school year). Prepare your students by having them research whales at their school or public library. Introduce the topic of endangered species.

Use one of the suggested Web sites to watch whales and have your students describe the experience in their journals. If you are using the school computer lab for this experience, divide the class into two groups with half researching whale information and the other half observing whales via the Web cam sites, then switch the groups.

Evaluation:
Students will experience the thrill of whale watching either by going on a whale watch or by using the Web.

Resources:
Welcome to Whale Net "A Day on a Whale Watch"
    <http://whale.wheelock.edu/whalenet-stuff/whalewatchsmyth.html>
EarthCam: Orca Cam
    <http://www.earthcam.com/usa/washington/sanjuanisland/>
OrcaCam
    <http://www.orcacam.com>

Celebrate Dinosaur Month

Subject: Science

Grade level: 2 to 5

Watch out. It's dinosaur month! Celebrate with a virtual Web museum visit to see Sue.

Activity Title:
Who's Sue?

Materials:
Web site access, suggested reading

Procedure:
Take your students on a virtual field trip to Chicago's Field Museum to visit the fossil of a Tyrannosaurus Rex. This virtual Web museum trip is a great example of how the resources of the world's best museums can be brought to your classroom. Studying dinosaurs is popular with students of all ages, so be prepared for the enthusiastic response of your class.

Evaluation:
Students will study dinosaur fossils and experience a virtual tour.

Resources:
Wahl, Jan. *The Field Mouse and the Dinosaur Named Sue*. New York: Scholastic, Inc., 2000.
Sue at the Field Museum
    <http://www.fmnh.org/suedefault.htm>

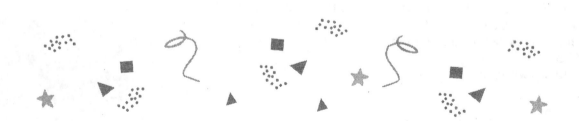

Celebrate Cookie Month

Subject: Language Arts

Grade level: K to 5

Home-baked cookies are becoming an endangered kitchen activity. Use this opportunity to teach how to follow written directions through recipe reading and writing.

Activity Title:

Mixed Up Cookies

Materials:

Student journals, whiteboard, recipe box prop, 3 x 5 cards

Procedure:

Locate a recipe for chocolate chip cookies and write the ingredients on the whiteboard. Write each sentence of the directions for preparing the cookies in the wrong order. Emphasize the importance of following directions in the right order in cooking. As a class, have the students put the directions in the correct sequence.

As a homework assignment have the students find a cookie recipe from a cookbook or from the Web to use as a penmanship lesson for their journals. Some recipes can be served on Valentine's Day.

Evaluation:

Students will learn the importance of following written directions by writing cookie recipes.

Resources:

Dahl, Roald. *Roald Dahl's Even More Revolting Recipes*. New York: Viking, 2001.
Thomas, John E. *The Ultimate Book for Holiday Kid Concoctions*. Strongsville, OH: Kids Concoction Co., 2001.

Celebrate National Pizza Month

Subject: Math

Grade level: K to 5

Celebrate National Pizza Month and National School Lunch Month by having a Pizza Party! Pizza parties are a favorite with elementary school students and a wonderful way to introduce or reinforce the math skills of pie charts, bar graphs, and surveys.

Activity Title:

Who Wants Pizza?

Materials:

Menus, posterboard, art materials, computer spreadsheet software

Procedure:

Gather menus from local pizza stores to use for price comparisons and kinds of toppings. Which one has the best prices? Which one has the pizza with the most varieties of toppings?

Divide the students into teams to design their own advertisement on a poster for the "Best Pizza in Town." Have another class critique the posters.

Evaluation:

Students will use a pizza theme to learn real-world math skills.

Resources:

Prelutsky, Jack. *A Pizza The Size of the Sun*. New York: Greenwillow Books, 1996.
Mrs. G's Kindergarten Pizza Unit
        <http://stafford.ctschool.net/BOROUGH/pizza.html>

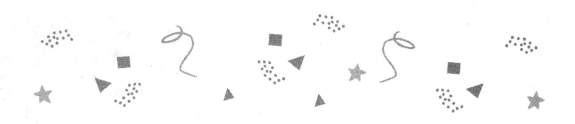

Celebrate United Nations Day

Subject: Social Studies

Grade level: 4 to 5

Celebrate the importance of the United Nations on its anniversary date of October 24.

Activity Title:
Celebrate Human Rights

Materials:

Web site access, student journals, whiteboard

Procedure:

Visit the student section of the Web site of the United Nations and have students find out the purpose of this organization.

Brainstorm with the class about the basic needs of all humans. What does every person need to survive? What values are necessary? Have the students reflect in their journals about the kind of world in which they want to live.

Evaluation:

Students will learn about the United Nations and its goals. Students will think about the issue of human rights and relate it to their own future.

Resources:

The United Nations: An Introduction for Students
    <http://www.un.org/Pubs/CyberSchoolBus/unintro/unintro.htm>
Understanding Human Rights
    <http://www0.un.org/cyberschoolbus/humanrights/about/understanding.asp>
What Kind of World Do I Want?
    <http://www.unac.org/kids/what_kind_of_world/>

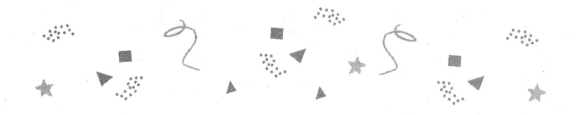

Celebrate National Dental Hygiene Month

Subject: Health

Grade level: K to 3

Promote a healthy attitude about dental hygiene by learning about tooth care.

Activity Title:

Smile!

Materials:

None

Procedure:

Invite a dentist or dental hygienist to visit the classroom and explain how students at your grade level can take care of their smile. Visit the suggested Web sites to find information to prepare your pre-visit lesson.

Evaluation:

Students will learn the importance of taking care of their teeth and gums and be introduced to careers in the field of medicine.

Resources:

Tooth Theme Day (K-2)
    <http://www.themeday.com/tooth_day.htm>
Healthy Teeth
    <http://healthyteeth.org>

Celebrate National Popcorn Popping Month

Subject: Social Studies

Grade level: 2 to 4

Celebrate National Popcorn Popping Month in October by learning about one of America's favorite year-round snacks and industries.

Activity Title:
Inside Out!

Materials:
Supplies to make popcorn in the classroom

Procedure:
Read *The Popcorn Book* by Tomie dePaola (or another book about popcorn) to point out interesting facts about the discovery of popcorn.

Explain how popcorn works. The unpopped kernel contains water inside. When the kernel is exposed to heat, the water expands and bursts the kernel inside out.

Enjoy eating the popcorn.

Use The Popcorn Board Web site to request your free teacher's packet!

Evaluation:
Students will learn about the history of popcorn from a favorite children's author and learn how popcorn works!

Resources:
De Paola, Tomie. *The Popcorn Book*. New York: Holiday House, 1978.
Moran, Alex. *Popcorn*. San Diego: Harcourt Brace & Company, 1999.
The Popcorn Board
    <http://www.popcorn.org>
A Day Full of Popcorn: An Ask ERIC K to 3 Lesson
    <http://ericir.syr.edu/Virtual/Lessons/Interdisciplinary/INT0015.html>
No Popcorn (at the First Thanksgiving)
    <http://www.plimoth.org/Library/Thanksgiving/nopopc.htm>

Celebrate Statue of Liberty Day

Subject: Social Studies, Language Arts
Grade level: 4 to 5

> The Statue of Liberty was dedicated on October 28, 1886, and designated as a national park on October 15, 1924. It is considered a symbol of democracy and political freedom for the whole world.

Activity Title:
Give Me Your Tired

Materials:
Web site access, copy of the poem by Emma Lazarus that appears on the Statue of Liberty

Procedure:
Visit the Statue of Liberty Web sites or use a book to display a photograph of the Statue. Discuss the meaning of the section of the poem "The New Colossus" that is inscribed on the statue.

Evaluation:
Students will deepen their understanding of the meaning of both past and present symbols of freedom.

Resources:
Statue of Liberty
    <http://www.greatbuildings.com/buildings/Statue-of-Liberty.htmls>
National Park Service: Statue of Liberty
    <http://www.nps.gov/stil>
The Invention Dimension: The Statue of Liberty
    <http://web.mit.edu/invent/www/inventorsI-Q/liberty.html>

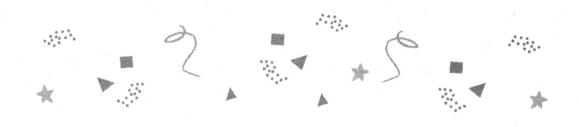

Celebrate Good Manners Day

Subject: Interdisciplinary

Grade level: K to 5

Celebrate good manners on Emily Post's birthday (October 30). Her name has been synonymous with good manners since she wrote a popular book dealing with etiquette many years ago.

Activity Title:
Behave Yourself

Materials:

Suggested reading, Web site access, whiteboard

Procedure:

With your students, brainstorm some ideas about good manners. Ask them if they have ever witnessed an adult or student whose behavior was inappropriate. If you are going to be using the Web with your students, explain that the rules of good manners apply there, too.

Evaluation:

Students will review the basics of good manners as they apply to the school and the community, and relate those to good manners when using the Internet.

Resources:

Ziegler, Sandra. *Manners*. Chicago: Children's Press, 1989.
The Core Rules of Netiquette
    <http://www.albion.com/netiquette/corerules.html>

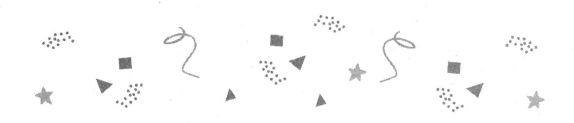

Celebrate Halloween

Subject: Interdisciplinary
Grade level: K to 5

Whether you celebrate the last day of October as Halloween, National Day of Magic, or as a celebration of the harvest, there's plenty of literature and Web-related resources for this time of year.

Activity Title:
Pumpkin Patch

Materials:

Very large pumpkin from a local farm, a few small pumpkins, a scale

Procedure:

Contact a local farm to make plans to pick up a very large pumpkin (but not so heavy that you can't carry it easily). Have it weighed and keep the weight a secret. Have the students guess the weight of the pumpkin as an estimation lesson. If possible, have a small scale with some smaller pumpkins for them to weigh as a comparison.

When all the estimation is done, carve or paint the pumpkin as a class project!

Evaluation:

Students will enjoy this fun fall holiday with their classmates.

Resources:

Halloweenkids.com: Celebrations Around the World
    <http://www.halloweenkids.com/k_world.htm>
North of Boston Library Exchange: Halloween
    <http://www.noblenet.org/year/tty10hal.htm>
Kids Domain: Halloween Resources
    <http://www.kidsdomain.com/holiday/halloween/index.html>

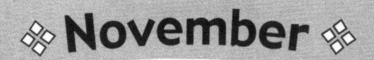
❖ November ❖

Activity 40:
Celebrate Dia de los Muertos

Subject: Interdisciplinary

Grade level: 3 to 4

Celebrate a traditional Mexican holiday to learn about ancient customs and beliefs.

Activity Title:
Day of the Dead

Materials:

Web site access, printed copy of Calaveras ("Skulls"). This is a traditional poem about the Day of the Dead. It is celebrated for three days—October 31, November 1, and 2.

Procedure:

Have the students learn the reason for celebrating this holiday and compare it to the American customs of Halloween. Print out the suggested poem and read it in Spanish or English to the class.

Connect this day to the arrival of the Monarch Butterflies in their overwintering locations in Mexico. What is the legend?

Evaluation:

Students will learn about an ancient celebration as celebrated in modern times.

Resources:

Joosse, Barbara. Ghost Wings. San Francisco: Chronicle Books, 2001.
NOBLE: El Dia de los Muertos
     <http://www.noblenet.org/year/tty11dia.htm>
Dia de Los Muertos Lessons for Elementary Students
     <http://star.ucc.nau.edu/FLI/DDLM/>
The Days of the Dead
     <http://www.i5ive.com/article.cfm/history_for_children/22803>

Celebrate National Author's Day

Subject: Reading

Grade level: 4 to 5

Celebrate National Author's Day learning about an author or an illustrator tied to your curriculum.

Activity Title:
Who Is the Author?

Materials:

Several different books by the same author, information sources about that author from print and the Web, Web site access

Procedure:

Check your school district's curriculum list of suggested authors and pick an author for your students to research.

Visit the school library media center or public library and use research skills to locate books written by that author and information about the author.

Read a book aloud or have the students read the books and share information about the life of that author.

Evaluation:

Students will learn about the life and work of an author.

Resources:

The Internet School Library Media Center: Index to Authors and Illustrators
    <http://falcon.jmu.edu/~ramseyil/biochildhome.htm>

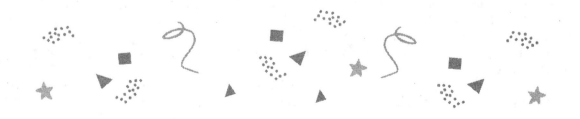

Activity 42:

Celebrate Sandwich Day

Subject: Health
Grade level: 3 to 5

Celebrate Sandwich Day on November 3 by preparing and eating sandwiches. The Earl of Sandwich, John Montague, invented the sandwich in 1762.

Activity Title:
Brown Bag Lunch

Materials:

Sandwich-making ingredients, plastic utensils, plastic sandwich bags, brown lunch bags, clean-up supplies

Procedure:

Your class will be preparing their own sandwiches, so make sure you have parent helpers on hand and materials to clean up the mess!

Brainstorm the ingredients needed to prepare a sandwich. As homework for the night before, have the students write those ingredients as a shopping list.

Have a student demonstrate making a sandwich as another student talks through the steps. Students can write the steps in their journals. They can then work as partners, with one student giving the directions and one following them exactly. After they make the sandwiches, they can eat them.

Evaluation:

Students will create a sandwich of their choice and learn to list the steps, in order, needed to make a sandwich.

Resources:

Upcoming Events on the Calendar: Sandwich Day Resources
    <http://www.umkc.edu/imc/sandwday.htm>

Activity 43:
Celebrate King Tut Day

Subject: Social Studies

Grade level: 4 to 5

> Celebrate the discovery of the tomb of the boy king, King Tutankhamen, who was Pharaoh of Egypt and only 18 years old when he died. His tomb was discovered on November 4, 1922.

Activity Title:
Everything Egypt

Materials:
Books on Egypt, Web site access

Procedure:
Everyone is fascinated with the world of Ancient Egypt. Even if your curriculum doesn't cover teaching about the ancient world, help your students develop an interest in this topic to encourage free reading time or as an idea for a whole-class project.

Evaluation:
Students will develop an interest in the Ancient World by learning about King Tut, the Pyramids, and the process of mummification.

Resources:
Donnelly, Judy. *Tut's Mummy Lost and Found*. New York: Random House, 1988.
Runhart, Edith. *Mummies*. New York: Golden Books, 2000.
Welcome to Ancient Egypt
    <http://www.geocities.com/sseagraves/ancientegyptlessonplans.htm>
WebQuest: King Tutankhamen: Was it Murder?
    <http://www.pekin.net/pekin108/wash/webquest/>
At the Tomb of Tutankhamen
    <http://www.nationalgeographic.com/egypt/>

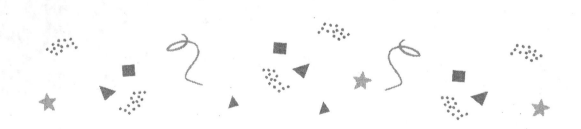

Celebrate John Philip Sousa's Birthday

Subject: Music

Grade level: 2 to 5

> Celebrate the life of John Philip Sousa, whose heart-stirring patriotic marches live on today. Born on November 6, 1854, Sousa also wrote some operettas. Have students understand that march music isn't just for parades; during wartime, bands also used march music to announce daily activities and commands.

Activity Title:
March Forever

Materials:

Audio CD or cassette of John Philip Sousa's marches, CD or cassette player with external speakers, Web site access with Real Player installed

Procedure:

Play Sousa's most popular march, "The Stars and Stripes Forever."

Have students brainstorm on which holiday they hear this played most often.

Evaluation:

Students will hear a march by an American composer and relate it to a personal Fourth of July experience.

Resources:

Venezia, Mike. *John Philip Sousa*. New York: Children's Press, 1998.
John Philip Sousa's The Stars and Strips Forever
    <http://www.dws.org/sousa/starsstripes.htm>

Celebrate Election Day

Subject: Social Studies

Grade level: 4 to 5

Celebrate Election Day (the first Tuesday on or after November 2) by learning about school, local city/town, or national elections.

Activity Title:

Vote!

Materials:

Whiteboard, Web site access

Procedure:

Voting is the essence of democracy and can be complicated to teach. Start by having a classroom election, perhaps to vote on studying a special unit (choosing an animal species to study can be popular). This will give you an opportunity to brainstorm a topic, have students write arguments, prepare a simple ballot, set up a voting station, vote, tally results, and declare a winner.

Use the suggested scavenger hunt page to demonstrate working through a Web scavenger hunt.

Evaluation:

Students will develop an awareness of the different kinds of elections that can be held in the community.

Resources:

Election Lessons by Linda C. Joseph
    <http://www.cyberbee.com/election/election.html>
Elementary Activities Web Scavenger Hunt by Linda C. Joseph
    <http://www.cyberbee.com/election/elem.html>
42Explore Topic: Elections
    <http://eduscapes.com/42explore/elect.htm>

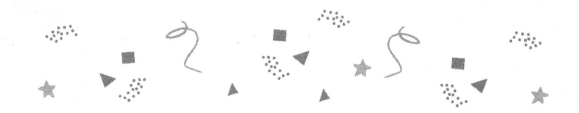

Activity 46:

Celebrate Veterans Day

Subject: Social Studies

Grade level: 4 to 5

Celebrate Veterans Day on November 11 by using the activities prepared for educators by the Veteran's Administration.

Activity Title:
Patriotic Planning

Materials:

Web site access

Procedure:

Visit the Web site and look for the prominently placed resources for the classroom. You can learn about this holiday, the history of our national anthem, and gun salutes and taps. Encourage your students to attend a local Veterans Day parade.

Evaluation:

Students will be exposed to the history of this holiday and learn about patriotism from the experts.

Resources:

Veterans Day Home Page
    <http://www.va.gov/pubaff/vetsday/index.htm>

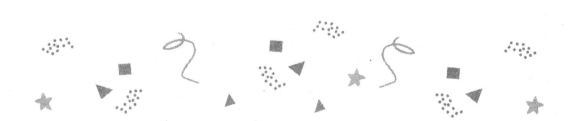

Celebrate Chemistry Week

Subject: Science

Grade level: 4 to 5

Chemistry is cool! Explore the life of a chemist and perform an experiment during the second week of November.

Activity Title:

Hot Chemistry

Materials:

Web site access

Procedure:

Visit the library to find some biographies of chemists similar to the suggested title. Emphasis for this activity should be placed on the connection among questioning, experimenting, invention, and hard work. Gertrude Elion is a Nobel Prize winner and the first woman to be named to the National Inventors Hall of Fame.

Find an easy chemistry experiment to perform in the classroom.

Evaluation:

Students will experience the exciting world of chemistry.

Resources:

St. Pierre, Stephanie. *Gertrude Elion: Master Chemist*. Vero Beach, FL: Rourke Enterprises, Inc., 1993.
Reeko's Mad Scientist Lab: Steel Wool Generating Heat
    <http://www.spartechsoftware.com/reeko/Experiments/ExpSteelWoolGeneratingHeat.htm>

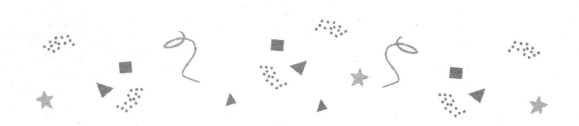

Celebrate Random Acts of Kindness

Subject: Character Education

Grade level: 3 to 5

Celebrate a week filled with random acts of kindness during the second week of November.

Activity Title:

Be Kind to Others

Materials:

Web site access, student journals, whiteboard

Procedure:

Being kind to others is a lifelong skill learned in childhood. Ask the students for their ideas on random acts of kindness and how this could be practiced in their lives.

As part of the journal activities for this month, ask the students to write about an experience of giving or receiving a random act of kindness.

Evaluation:

Students will be able to identify random acts of kindness and practice them for a week.

Resources:

The Random Acts of Kindness Foundation
     <http://www.actsofkindness.org/free_resources/activity_ideas.html>

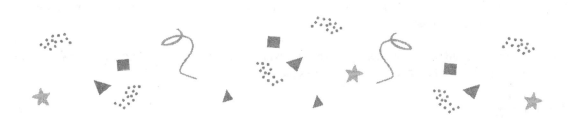

Celebrate National Children's Book Week

Subject: Reading

Grade level: 4 to 5

> National Children's Book Week is an annual event occurring in the second week of November devoted to inspiring young people to read.

Activity Title:

Read Along with Harry by Kathleen Wasik

Materials:

Bulletin board supplies, Mini-Book Report Forms, reward coupons, supplies and food for the party

Procedure:

Prepare a bulletin board for this activity with some Harry Potter artwork and a "broomstick" replica (created with construction paper) with an oaktag handle. Mark the handle with incentive marks, one for each ten books, to a total of one hundred books. Place two large envelopes on the bulletin board, one for blank book reports forms and one for completed forms. The master Mini-Book Report Form can be decorated with student-created artwork, such as an owl motif for this Harry Potter theme. Reproduce enough report forms for one hundred books. (This activity can be easily adapted to other children's book themes.)

Explain the reading incentive program to the students. Students will choose fiction or nonfiction chapter books of their choice from the classroom, school library media center, or public library. For each book read, the student will take one blank mini-report form from its envelope, fill it out as directed by the teacher, and place it in the finished report envelope. The teacher will read each book report and mark its completion on the broom handle.

After each two books read, with teacher approval, a reward coupon is given to the student. When the class goal of one hundred books has been read, the class has a party.

Evaluation:

Students will use this week to begin a yearlong book reading incentive program in the classroom. (Younger students can use this activity with modification.)

Resources:

Owl Mail: Harry Potter Thematic Resources for Education
  <http://www.midgefrazel.net/owlmail.html>

Celebrate National Geography Awareness Week

Subject: Interdisciplinary

Grade level: 3 to 5

Celebrate the importance of geography to the classroom during National Geography Awareness Week, which is held the week before Thanksgiving.

Activity Title:
Where Is Home?

Materials:
Atlas, maps, encyclopedias, local history books, local experts on geography

Procedure:
Depending on the area in which you live, plan a course of study on the landforms, habitats, or biomes and link these to your curriculum. This study can move across the disciplines and increase your students' awareness of their town's or state's geography. The project can be presented on National Geography Day.

Evaluation:
Students will begin a yearlong study of local geography.

Resources:
National Geography Awareness Week
<http://www.nationalgeographic.com/gaw/about.html>

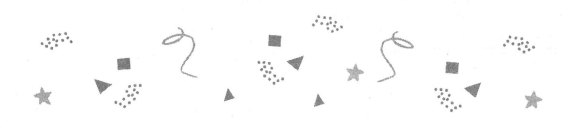

Celebrate Robert Louis Stevenson's Birthday

Subject: Reading, Language Arts

Grade level: 5

> Celebrate the Birthday of Robert Louis Stevenson on November 13.

Activity Title:
Shadows

Materials:

Copy of *A Child's Garden of Verses* in print or online, Web site access

Procedure:

Have the students read and analyze "My Shadow." How does a shadow "go in and out with me"? What's an India-rubber ball or a nursie? Tell the students about Stevenson's childhood illnesses and how his wonderful imagination led to the creation of his adventure stories.

Ask the students to find out about other writings of Stevenson, such as *Treasure Island*. Much of his work is in electronic format and can be read on the Web for free.

Evaluation:

Students will analyze Stevenson's poem "My Shadow."

Resources:

Stevenson, Robert Louis. *A Child's Garden of Verses*. Nashville: Tommy Nelson, 1999.
My Shadow by R.L. Stevenson
    <http://www.bartleby.com/188/119.html>
Robert Louis Stevenson Web Site
    <http://www.unibg.it/rls/rls.htm>

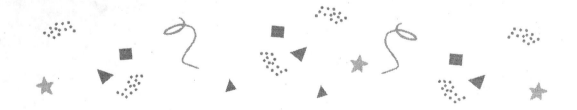

Celebrate Claude Monet's Birthday

Subject: Art, Science

Grade level: 5

> Celebrate Monet's birthday with a study of Impressionist paintings and their relationship to the science of light and color.

Activity Title:
Light and Color

Materials:
Books or Web sites with reproductions of Monet's paintings

Procedure:
Prior to looking at Monet's work, students should learn about the color wheel.

Ask the art teacher to visit the classroom and work with the students to teach primary and secondary colors.

Have the students examine one of Monet's paintings to get an impression of how light and color define the Impressionist era.

Connect this to the study of light in science.

Evaluation:
Students will learn about art and its close relationship to science.

Resources:
Explore Monet's World
    <http://www.mfa.org/monetsworld/>
Light and Color at the Franklin Institute
    <http://www.fi.edu/color/color.html>

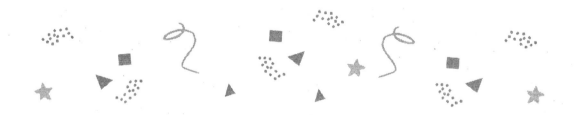

Celebrate American Education Week

Subject: Social Studies, Language Arts
Grade level: 4 to 5

> Celebrate American Education Week (the week prior to the week of Thanksgiving) by learning about your school.

Activity Title:
My School

Materials:
History of the school district/building, Web site access

Procedure:
Have your students research the history of the school by finding out when it was built, how many principals it has had, and whether any teachers presently in the building were teaching (or even alive!) when the school was built. An interesting idea is to find out if multiple generations of students have come from one family. Some of this information is available from the school committee, the administration building, the town hall, the public library, or even the school district's home page.

Evaluation:
Students will learn about the history of their school building.

Resources:
American Education Week
    <http://www.nea.org/aew/>

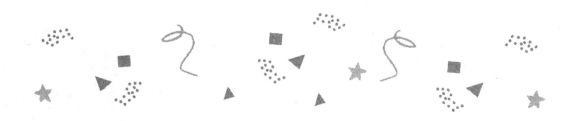

Celebrate Jean Fritz's Birthday

Subject: Reading

Grade level: 3 to 5

Celebrate the birthday of children's author Jean Fritz on November 16 with a reading of her book on the adventures of Plymouth Rock.

Activity Title:
That's Plymouth Rock?

Materials:
Suggested book by the author, Web site access

Procedure:

Read *Who's That Stepping on Plymouth Rock?* on Jean Fritz's birthday or as a Thanksgiving week activity.

Experience the Web presentation created by the author of this book. There are digital images of the rock and links to historically significant writings from Plimoth Plantation.

Discuss the symbolism of this unimpressive, but important, first symbol of America. How do the Native Americans feel about Thanksgiving?

Evaluation:

Students will learn about a symbol of America and understand its relevance to today's world.

Resources:
Fritz, Jean. *Who's That Stepping on Plymouth Rock?* New York: Putnam and Grossett Group, 1975.
Carol Hurst's Author Study: Jean Fritz
    <http://www.carolhurst.com/authors/jfritz.html>
That's Plymouth Rock? Web Presentation
    <http://www.midgefrazel.net/rocksld1.html>

Celebrate National Family Week

Subject: Interdisciplinary
Grade level: 4 to 5

Celebrate National Family Week during the third week of November by learning about genealogy and the practice of recording family history.

Activity Title:
Close and Distant Family

Materials:

Sample genealogy charts or simple family trees, student journals, Web site access

Procedure:

Digging for family roots is a growing interest for users of the Web. Students, even those with nontraditional families, can benefit from learning the structure of generations. Have your students learn to record the names of their parents, grandparents, and great-grandparents. Some students may choose to record their adoptive or foster parents, or research the family of a famous person.

Evaluation:

Students will be able to identify multiple generations of family and learn about maternal and paternal roots.

Resources:

Genealogy Spot for Kids
<http://www.genealogyspot.com/features/kids.htm>
Family Tree Graphic Organizer
<http://www.sdcoe.k12.ca.us/score/actbank/tfamtree.htm>
Celebrity Family Trees
<http://www.genealogy.com/famousfolks/index.html>

Celebrate Stamp Collecting

Subject: Art, Social Studies

Grade level: 4 to 5

Celebrate this day (November 17) with the Stamp Collectors Society of America by learning about the lives of important historical figures on stamps.

Activity Title:
Portrait of a Stamp

Materials:

Reproducible: Activity 56: Design a Stamp, Web site access, stamp collection

Procedure:

Stamp collecting is a multigenerational hobby, so it may not be hard to find a parent or grandparent with a stamp collection for display in the classroom. Schedule a field trip to the local post office, which has materials for students to learn about the United States Post Office.

Have your students design their own stamp (Reproducible: Activity 56: Design a Stamp) and write a description of the person or event depicted on their design.

Evaluation:

Students will learn about United States postage stamps.

Resources:

Teaching with Stamps
    <http://www.richmond.edu/~pstohrhu/stamps/>
American Philatelic Society: Kids
    <http://www.stamps.org/kids/kid_StampFun.htm>

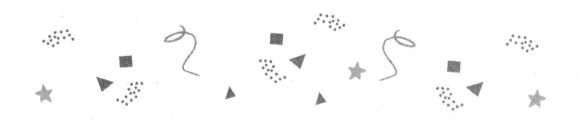

Activity 56: Design a Stamp

Name _____

Name _____

Celebrate Mickey Mouse's Birthday

Subject: Art

Grade level: 3 to 4

Celebrate the art of animation on the birthday of the most famous mouse in the world. Walt Disney created Mickey on November 18, 1928, in a short cartoon entitled "Steamboat Willie." Here are some names for Mickey in other languages: (France) Michel Souris, (Japan) Miki Kuchi, (Spain) Miguel Ratonocito, and (Denmark) Mikkel Mus.

Activity Title:
Mickey's Famous Face

Materials:
Art supplies, Web site access

Procedure:
Students draw Mickey Mouse from a tutorial on the Disney Web site.

If no Web access is available, have students use graph paper to reproduce a picture of Mickey.

Evaluation:
Students will learn about the most famous cartoon character in the world by learning about the art of cartooning.

Resources:
Let's Draw Mickey Activity
    <http://disney.go.com/DisneyBooks/activities/1560100877.html?id=2110>

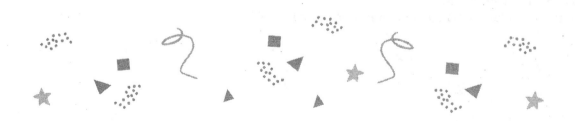

Celebrate Thanksgiving

Subject: Social Studies, Language Arts

Grade level: K to 5

Celebrate Thanksgiving with factual information about the First Thanksgiving in America.

Activity Title:

Giving Thanks

Materials:

Web site access, student journals

Procedure:

Visit the Web pages of Plimoth Plantation and gather facts about the event. Have the students look at the famous painting and decide if it is an accurate depiction of the event. What do the Native Americans (National Day of Mourning) think of the depiction of this event? The Plimoth Plantation Kid's Page has wonderful activities to be printed and used in the classroom.

Have the students write about something they are thankful for in their student journals. You may wish to brainstorm ideas with your students to focus their attention away from the distractions of the upcoming holiday season.

Evaluation:

Students will learn about the First Thanksgiving and the different perspectives of the historical events

Resources:

Plimoth Plantation: Thanksgiving
    <http://www.plimoth.org/Library/Thanksgiving/thanksgi.htm>
Plimouth Plantation Kids Page
    <http://www.plimoth.org/Education/kidspage.htm>
Kids Domain: Thanksgiving
    <http://www.kidsdomain.com/holiday/thanks/index.html>

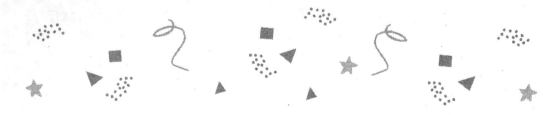

Celebrate Marc Brown's Birthday

Subject: Reading

Grade level: K to 4

> Everyone can empathize with the world-famous aardvark, Arthur, his friends, and family. Celebrate Marc Brown's birthday (November 25, 1948) with a reading of one of his books.

Activity Title:
Aardvark Fever!

Materials:
Web site access, books by the author

Procedure:
Connect this celebration to the season with a reading of one of Marc Brown's books.

Visit the Web site for ideas and activities for your students.

Evaluation:
Students will celebrate the author's birthday with readings of his works.

Resources:
Brown, Marc. *Arthur's Thanksgiving*. Boston: Little, Brown, 1983.
Arthur, The World's Most Famous Aardvark
   <http://www.pbs.org/wgbh/arthur/>

Celebrate Kevin Henkes' Birthday

Subject: Reading, Writing

Grade level: K

> Celebrate the birthday of Kevin Henkes on November 27 with a special reading of his popular book about Lilly and her adventures in kindergarten.

Activity Title:

Lilly's Writing Workshop by Heather Frazel

Materials:

Lilly's Purple Plastic Purse by Kevin Henkes, chart paper, alphabet strip (to refer to for sounds), pencils, crayons, 11 x 14 inch white construction paper (durable)

Procedure:

Read the book *Lilly's Purple Plastic Purse* by Kevin Henkes.

Discuss and define with the students "What is a job?"

Ask the children to close their eyes and think about what they would like to be when they grow up (review ideas from the story). Tell the children to open their eyes when they have their idea.

Brainstorm and record the students' ideas on chart paper. Allow the students to help sound out the spelling of the title of the job as you record their ideas.

Pass out a sheet of paper to each student. Ask the students to use "all of their words" to complete the sentence starter "When I grow up I want to be a _____."

Have students gather as a whole group to share their work.

An additional idea is to create a class book with the students' work to send home.

Evaluation:

Students will begin basic writing skills.

Resources:

Henkes, Kevin. *Lilly's Purple Plastic Purse*. New York: Greenwillow Books, 1996.
Lilly's Plastic Purse Activities Page
    <http://www.harperchildrens.com/hch/picture/series/lilly/>
Lilly's Plastic Purse Literature Guide by Nancy Polette
    <http://www.nancypolette.com/LitGuidesText/LillysPurplePlasticPurse.htm>

December

Activity 61:

Celebration of Light

Subject: Interdisciplinary
Grade level: 2 to 5

Celebrate December holidays with the theme of light.

Activity Title:
Festivals of Light

Materials:
Web site access, books on the topic

Background information:

Kwanzaa is celebrated on December 26 by lighting the first candle on a candleholder called the kinara. The first candle is black (unity) and is placed in the center. Six other candles, three red (struggle for freedom and equality) are placed to the left, and three green (hope for the future) are placed to the right.

During Chanukah, nine candles are lit to celebrate the oil lasting in the temple for eight days when there was only enough oil for one day. The candleholder is called the menorah, and the ninth candle is used to light the other candles, one each night.

Christians use lighted candles on Christmas trees and on windowsills during the time before, during, and after Christmas Day to symbolize the light of the star of Bethlehem.

Procedure:

Ask parents to help with these seasonal activities. Learning about the seasonal religious ceremonies of December is an important home-school connection.

Most major celebrations revolve around the lighting of candles or lanterns, and parents can bring the candles and holders into the classroom.

Teach older students about candle safety and a science lesson on the properties of light.

Evaluation:
Students will learn about the celebration of candle lighting in several seasonal holidays.

Resources:

Festival of Light
      <http://teacherlink.ed.usu.edu/TLresources/longterm/LessonPlans/Byrnes/light.html>
Kids Domain: Christmas, Chanukah and Kwanzaa
      <http://www.kidsdomain.com/holiday/xmas/index.html>
      <http://www.kidsdomain.com/holiday/chanukah/index.html>
      <http://www.kidsdomain.com/holiday/kwanzaa/index.html>
Ben and Jerry Winter Holidays
      <http://www.benjerry.com/yule/index.html>

Celebrate National Calendar Awareness Month

Subject: Interdisciplinary

Grade level: K to 5

Celebrate December as National Calendar Awareness Month by strengthening your students' knowledge of calendar skills. Remembering and recording information is a life skill. Strengthen your math units with a calendar-making celebration.

Activity Title:
Dates to Remember

Materials:

Blank calendars (created by hand drawing, using a computer application, or found on the Web), Web site access, encyclopedias (print, CD-ROM, or Web-based)

Procedure:

Have the students create a calendar for the upcoming year. Younger students will learn the names of the months and weeks of the year. Older students will learn to record personal achievements, family birthdays, and important state and federal holidays.

You may wish your students to use this activity to begin a multicultural unit or as a famous days in history or science activity. Groups of students could focus on different celebrations and report to the class each month for the rest of the school year.

Evaluation:

Students in all grades will reinforce their calendar skills.

Resources:

Eduplace: Make a Multicultural Calendar
    <http://www.eduplace.com/ss/act/calend.html>
EnchantedLearning.com: A to Z Calendar Printouts
    <http://www.enchantedlearning.com/calendar/>

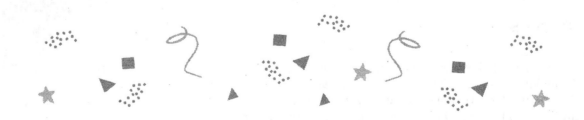

Celebrate Gingerbread Month

Subject: Reading, Language Arts

Grade level: K to 2

Celebrate the birthday of children's author Jan Brett on December 1 with a gingerbread day.

Activity Title:
Gingerbread Birthday

Materials:
Suggested readings, Web site access, gingerbread

Procedure:
Start out December with a reading of the classic folktale of the Gingerbread Man as retold in Jan Brett's delightful *Gingerbread Baby*.

Prepare gingerbread or gingerbread "men" cookies for after the reading. Jan Brett's Web site has several activities that complement this book.

Evaluation:
Students will listen to traditional retellings of folktales and enjoy eating gingerbread.

Resources:
Brett, Jan. *Gingerbread Baby*. New York: G.P. Putnam's Sons, 1999.
Aylesworth, Jim. *The Gingerbread Man*. New York: Scholastic Press, 1998.
Jan Brett's Gingerbread Baby Board Game
     <http://www.janbrett.com/games/gingerbread_baby_board_game.htm>
Jan Brett's Gingerbread Animals Masks
     <http://www.janbrett.com/gingerbread_baby_masks_main.htm>
TeacherView: Gingerbread Baby
     <http://www.eduplace.com/tview/pages/g/Gingerbread_Baby_Jan_Brett.html>

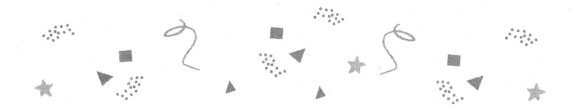

Celebrate Gilbert Stuart's Birthday

Subject: Art, Social Studies

Grade level: 5

Celebrate the birthday (December 3, 1755) of American portrait painter Gilbert Stuart by learning about portrait painting.

Activity Title:

Before the Camera

Materials:

Web site access, student journals

Procedure:

Explain that before the invention of the camera, the only way to record what a famous person looked like was to have a portrait painted. Gilbert Stuart was one of the first American portrait painters.

Have the students examine portraits of George Washington in print or on the Web. Is this what President Washington really looked like? Did the artist get paid more if the painting was more flattering?

Have students write about pictures created by artists before the invention of the camera.

Evaluation:

Students will examine portraits of George Washington painted by Gilbert Stuart and others, and reflect on the impressions of portrait paintings.

Resources:

Portraits of George Washington
    <http://www.virginia.edu/gwpapers/maps/index.html>#portraits>
Gilbert Stuart's Birthplace
    <http://www.loc.gov/bicentennial/propage/RI/ri-2_h_weygand4.html>

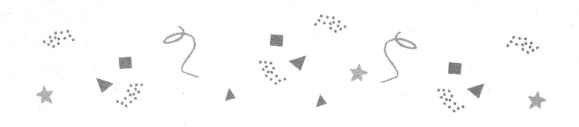

Celebrate Polar Bear Month

Subject: Interdisciplinary
Grade level: 2 to 5

Celebrate winter animals by using an interdisciplinary unit from the Web on polar bears.

Activity Title:
Life in the Arctic

Materials:

Web site access

Procedure:

Gander Academy has a great resource that makes it easy to learn to use a Web-based lesson. With support pages, activity sheets, and research Web pages, your students will quickly learn about the environment, habitat, and life of the polar bear.

If your students are in grades 2 or 3, there is a special Web page with resources for younger students.

Evaluation:

Students will learn to use a Web-based theme lesson.

Resources:

Gander Academy's Polar Bears Theme Page
    <http://www.stemnet.nf.ca/CITE/polar_bears.htm>

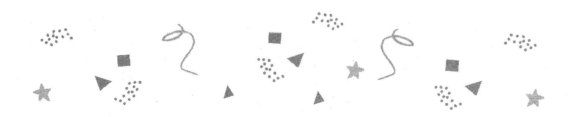

Celebrate Letter Writing Day

Subject: Writing

Grade level: 3 to 5

Celebrate Letter Writing Day by learning the correct method for addressing envelopes.

Activity Title:
The Envelope, Please

Materials:

Reproducible Activity 66: Envelope Addressing Graphic Organizer, student journals

Procedure:

December is the busiest month for the United States Postal Service. Teach your students the correct method for addressing an envelope and for using a return address. (Use Reproducible Activity 66: Envelope Addressing Graphic Organizer.) This is an opportunity to teach the abbreviations for each state. Many students will be writing thank-you notes for gifts received this month, and addressing the envelope is a necessary skill.

Evaluation:

Students will learn the skill of addressing an envelope.

Resources:

U.S.P.S. Envelope Addressing
    <http://www.academic.uofs.edu/department/MAILING_SERVICES/Addressing.HTML>
ABCteach Envelope Example
    <http://www.abcteach.com/Writing/envelope.htm>

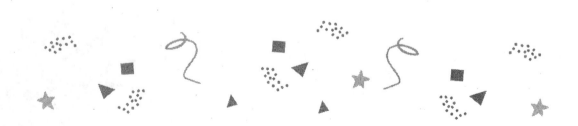

Activity 66: Envelope Addressing Graphic Organizer

Name _____

Name _____

Celebrate Aurora Borealis Day

Subject: Art, Science

Grade level: 5

> Celebrate the first recorded viewing of the Aurora Borealis on December 11, 1719, by learning about "the paintings in the sky."

Activity Title:
Art in the Sky

Materials:

Web site access, colored chalk, black construction paper

Procedure:

After learning about the aurora borealis, have the students create aurora art by using different color chalk drawings on black construction paper.

If weather permits, this type of smudged chalk drawings also can be done on the asphalt of the school playground.

Evaluation:

Students will learn about the Northern Lights and create a chalk drawing.

Resources:

The Aurora Explained
    <http://www.alaskascience.com/aurora.htm>
Auroras: Paintings in the Sky
    <http://www.exploratorium.edu/learning_studio/auroras/index.html>

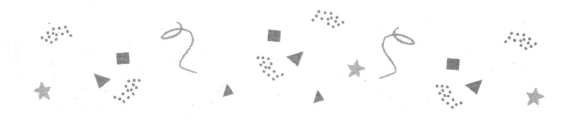

Celebrate Winter Safety Day

Subject: Interdisciplinary

Grade level: 2 to 5

> Celebrate Winter Safety Day with a whole-class discussion dealing with safety at school and at home in the winter months.

Activity Title:
Ice and Snow: Be Safe!

Materials:

Whiteboard, student journals, Web site access

Procedure:

Winter can be a challenge in many states. The darkness of December, January, and February can be hazardous to those children who walk to school or wait in large groups for the school bus. Brainstorm with your class some winter safety tips, including ice safety.

Your local police and fire departments may have materials for winter weather preparedness to share with your school.

Evaluation:

Students will be aware of safety issues before, during, and after school.

Resources:

Winter Safety
    <http://itre.ncsu.edu/GHSP/winter.html>

Celebrate Bill of Rights Day

Subject: Social Studies

Grade level: 5

Celebrate December 15, 1791, the day the first ten amendments to our Constitution were ratified.

Activity Title:
Ten Basic Freedoms

Materials:

Copy of the Bill of Rights (paper or electronic), Web site access

Procedure:

Look for the Bill of Rights in your encyclopedia or in the National Archives online. Choose one of the rights to discuss with the class.

Ask them to write their thoughts in their student journals.

Evaluation:

Students will explore our freedoms from the Bill of Rights.

Resources:

The Bill of Rights
    <http://www.nara.gov/exhall/charters/billrights/billmain.html>
Celebrations Mini-Unit: Bill of Rights Day
    <http://teacherlink.ed.usu.edu/TLresources/longterm/LessonPlans/Byrnes/billrigh.html>

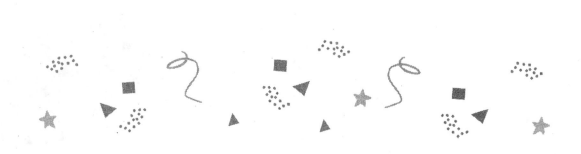

Celebrate Basketball Invention Month

Subject: Physical Education

Grade level: 4 to 5

Celebrate a popular sport by learning about its inventor. Dr. James Naismith invented the game of basketball in December of 1891.

Activity Title:

Hoops

Materials:

Basketball, playground, Web site access

Procedure:

Students can learn powerful lessons by studying a sport. Ask the students to learn, practice, and demonstrate a skill of this game.

Have students use the Web sites listed to learn about the invention of this American sport.

Evaluation:

Students will learn the history of a sport and plan a demonstration of skill.

Resources:

Kansas Sports Hall of Fame: James Naismith
    <http://www.kshof.org/inductees/naismith.html>
Skills and Drills
    <http://members.aol.com/msdaizy/sports/skills2.html>
Basketball Goal Book
    <http://www.abcteach.com/MonthtoMonth/December/basketball.htm>

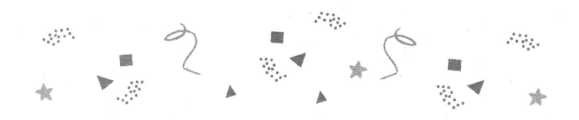

Celebrate Flight at Kitty Hawk Day

Subject: Social Studies, Science
Grade level: 4 to 5

> Celebrate the first powered flight, which took place on December 17, 1903, by the Wright Brothers.

Activity Title:
Soar!

Materials:
Web site access, student journals

Procedure:
Have students design paper airplanes and fly them in the school gym or, weather permitting, outside. Students can share ideas in groups and compete to make the best paper airplane.

As a writing activity, students can write the steps taken to fold the airplanes and see if another student can follow those written directions.

Evaluation:
Students will learn about the beginnings of flight and the close relationship between two brothers.

Resources:
Robinson, Nick. *Super Simple Paper Airplanes*. New York: Sterling Publishing Co., 1998.
Flights of Inspiration
    <http://www.fi.edu/flights/index.html>
Flights Of Inspiration: Teacher's Guide Resources
    <http://www.fi.edu/flights/teacher/hotlist.html>
Alex's Paper Airplanes
    <http://www.paperairplanes.co.uk/>

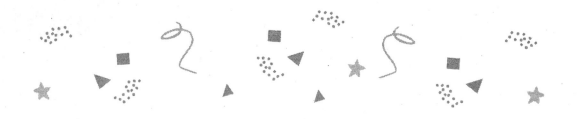

Celebrate the Boston Tea Party Day

Subject: Social Studies

Grade level: 4 to 5

Celebrate The Boston Tea Party that took place on December 16, 1773, with research on this event of the Revolutionary War.

Activity Title:

Boycott

Materials:

Suggested readings, Web site access, encyclopedias (print, CD-ROM, or Web-based)

Procedure:

What is a symbolic gesture? What is a boycott? Why didn't the colonists just grow their own tea? These are some of the critical thinking questions that your students can research to celebrate the dumping of the tea into Boston Harbor.

Evaluation:

Students will do research on an important event in American history.

Resources:

Hull, Mary E. *The Boston Tea Party*. Springfield, NJ: Easlow Publishers, Inc., 1999.
Stein, R. Conrad. *Cornerstones of Freedom: The Boston Tea Party*. New York: Children's Press, 1997.
Boston Tea Party A to Z History
      <http://school.discovery.com/homeworkhelp/worldbook/atozhistory/b/071320.html>
The Boston Tea Party Ship and Museum
      <http://www.bostonteapartyship.com/>

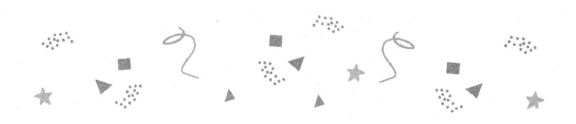

Celebrate Beethoven's Birthday

Subject: Music, Science

Grade level: 4 to 5

> Celebrate the Birthday (December 17, 1770) of Ludwig van Beethoven, a classical composer who wrote some of his best work while deaf.

Activity Title:

Hear the Symphony

Materials:

Web site access, Real Player or audio cassette or CD player with speakers

Procedure:

Visit the Web site to listen to short clips of the composer's music, or listen to a cassette or audio CD of his music.

Have the students feel the vibrations produced by music by putting their hands on the speaker of the cassette player.

Have the students investigate deafness. While listening to different pieces created by this brilliant man, they can reflect on the effects on life of being deaf in their student journals.

Evaluation:

Students will learn about the composer Ludwig Van Beethoven.

Resources:

Deafness A to Z Science
<http://school.discovery.com/homeworkhelp/worldbook/atozscience/d/150560.html>

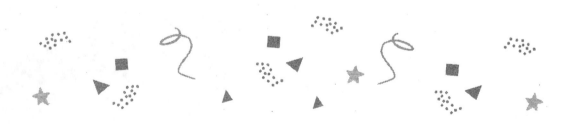

Celebrate Earmuffs Invention Day

Subject: Science, Art, Language Arts

Grade level: 3 to 4

Celebrate Earmuffs Invention Day on December 21 by inventing your own earmuffs design.

Activity Title:

Warm Ears

Materials:

Art materials, earmuffs, beads, feathers, ribbons, other decorations

Procedure:

Schools located in climates that are warm in December may find this a strange assignment, but students will enjoy imagining having to keep their ears warm in cold weather. Have students draw the kind of earmuffs they would like to wear to protect their ears. Some students may like to add beads or ribbons to their real earmuffs.

Fashion design is not always practical, so have students brainstorm what decorations will be affected adversely by the winter weather.

Tie this activity into the curriculum by defining invention and innovation.

Evaluation:

Students will learn to design an article of clothing.

Resources:

42Explore Topic: Inventors and Inventions
        <http://eduscapes.com/42explore/invent.htm>

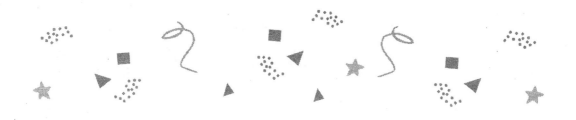

Celebrate the First Day of Winter

Subject: Reading, Science
Grade level: K to 1

Celebrate the first day of winter on December 21 or 22 (depending on the year) with an activity related to snow.

Activity Title:
Winter Wonderland

Materials:

Snow, plastic bags, suggested reading

Procedure:

Read *The Snowy Day* aloud to the class.

Have the students put a handful of snow in a plastic bag and bring it into the classroom. What happened to the snow when it was brought inside?

Evaluation:

Students will learn about prediction by listening to a book that won the 1963 Caldecott Medal.

Resources:

Keats, Ezra Jack. *The Snowy Day*. New York: Viking Press, 1996.
Snow/Water Ice
    <http://www.minnetonka.k12.mn.us/science/lessonsk1/snow.html>
TeacherView: The Snowy Day
    <http://www.eduplace.com/tview/pages/s/The_Snowy_Day_Ezra_Jack_Keats.html>
Winter Theme
    <http://www.teacherfeatures.com/themes/winter_theme.htm>

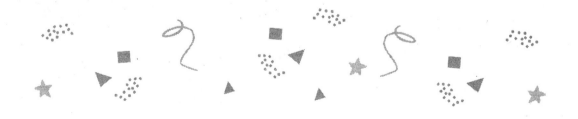

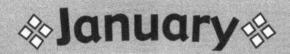

Activity 76:

Celebrate the New Year

Subject: Language Arts

Grade level: 1 to 5

Have students understand that it is traditional to celebrate a new year by making resolutions.

Activity Title:
New Beginnings

Materials:

Student journals

Procedure:

As a journal writing activity to start the New Year, ask your students to define resolution.

Brainstorm some resolutions with them and ask them to use reflective journaling to write about a self-improvement goal.

Have them review the learning goal they made at the beginning of the school year. Do they feel that their resolutions will last?

Evaluation:

Students will reflect on self-improvement in the classroom, home, and community.

Resources:

Auld Lang Syne
    <http://www.wilstar.com/xmas/auldlangsyne.htm>

Celebrate Louis Braille's Birthday

Subject: Science, Language Arts
Grade level: 4 to 5

Celebrate the invention of Braille by learning about the life of Louis Braille, who was born on January 4. This date is often called World Braille Day.

Activity Title:
Raised Dots

Materials:

Reproducible Activity 77: Braille Alphabet Graphic Organizer, suggested books, Web site access

Procedure:

Have the students learn about the childhood of Louis Braille, how he became blind, where he went to school, and how he invented Braille. Create a classroom project about blindness.

If you have Web site access, visit the suggested Web sites, finding the resources for your students to experiment with reading and writing Braille. Because there are many books in print about Braille, your library also may have some of them. See if your school district has access to a Braille typewriter or printer.

In the student journals, have students reflect on what it would be like for them to live their life without sight. Use the Reproducible Activity 77: Braille Alphabet Graphic Organizer to have students write their first name in Braille.

Evaluation:

Students will learn how the Braille alphabet works and how it changed the lives of the blind.

Resources:

Birch, Beverly. *Louis Braille*. Milwaukee: Gareth Stevens Children's Books, 1989.
Bryant, Jennifer Fisher. *Louis Braille*. New York: Chelsea House Publishers, 1994.
About Braille and Moon
    <http://www.rnib.org.uk/braille/welcome.htm>
World Braille Day School Activity Kit
    <http://www.cnib.ca/wbu/braille_day/students/braille.htm>
Write Your Name in Braille
    <http://www.hotbraille.com/>
General Braille Information
    <http://disserv3.stu.umn.edu/ALTFORM/brail-top.html>

Activity 77: Braille Alphabet Graphic Organizer

Name _____

Braille Alphabet

a	b	c	d	e	f
g	h	i	j	k	l
m	n	o	p	q	r
s	t	u	v	w	x
y	z				

Write Your Name in Braille

Celebrate Isaac Newton's Birthday

Subject: Science, Mathematics

Grade level: 5

Celebrate the work of other great scientists and mathematicians on Isaac Newton's Birthday (January 4, 1642). Sir Isaac Newton's greatest inventions were the reflecting telescope, the invention of calculus, and the Three Laws of Motion.

Activity Title:
Prisms

Materials:
Prism, sunlight, blank wall

Procedure:
Demonstrate the rainbow that is made when light passes through a glass prism.

Use the Web site on color to teach about refraction.

Evaluation:
Students will understand the rainbow created by the refraction of light.

Resources:
McTavish, Douglas. *Isaac Newton*. New York: The Bookwright Press, 1990.
Isaac Newton
    <http://www.pbs.org/wnet/hawking/cosmostar/html/cstars_newt.html>
Make a Splash with Color
    <http://www.thetech.org/exhibits_events/online/color/light/>

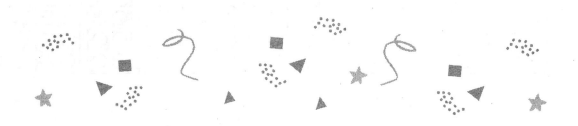

Celebrate Dia de Reyes

Subject: Interdisciplinary
Grade level: 3 to 5

Celebrate this traditional Mexican holiday by learning about the story of the visit of the Three Kings.

Activity Title:
Journey

Materials:
Student journals, whiteboard

Procedure:

Tell the story of the three kings who traveled through the desert, guided only by a star, to bring gifts to Bethlehem. Use one of the suggested readings to help tell the story. Explain how religious customs are part of our heritage.

Use the whiteboard to brainstorm key words on "adventure," "journey," and the "unknown."

Use the student journals to have the students reflect on venturing to an unknown location.

Evaluation:
Students will reflect on venturing into the unknown.

Resources:

Carlson, Lori Marie. *Hurray for the Three Kings*. New York: Morrow Junior Books, 1999.
Kanellos, Nicholas, ed. Noche Buena: Hispanic American Christmas Stories. New York: Oxford University Press, 2000.
Ya Vienen Los Reyes Magos!
    <http://www.inside-mexico.com/ReyesMagos.htm>

Celebrate Joan of Arc's Birthday

Subject: Interdisciplinary

Grade level: 5

> Learn about the courage of a young girl named Joan of Arc, whose strong beliefs made her famous. She was born on January 6 in France around the year 1412.

Activity Title:
Courage and Vision

Materials:
Biography of Joan of Arc

Procedure:

Tell students that Joan's heroism saved a whole country from defeat. She never went to school and could not read or write, but her strong religious beliefs gave her the courage to fight alongside men in battle. She was burned at the stake after she was charged with being a witch.

Have the students reflect on the story in their journals and answer the question "Would you be brave enough to stand up to a king?"

Evaluation:
Students will learn about the courage and conviction of a young girl.

Resources:

Hodges, Margaret. *Joan of Arc: The Lily Maid*. New York: Holiday House, 1999.
Discovery School's A to Z History: Joan of Arc.
     <http://school.discovery.com/homeworkhelp/worldbook/atozhistory/j/288800.html>

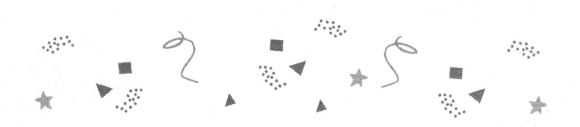

Celebrate International Thank You Day

Subject: Language Arts, Math
Grade level: 4 to 5

Thank you! It doesn't take much to say it, but it is often the most appreciated two words in any language. Celebrate it on International Thank You Day on January 11.

Activity Title:
Grazie

Materials:
Foreign language dictionaries, Web site access

Procedure:
Have your students find out how to write "thank you" in different languages by using dictionaries or Web sites.

Have students keep track of the number of times the words "thanks" or thank you" are said in the classroom each day for a week. Have them graph the results.

Evaluation:
Students will learn to write "thank you" in different languages.

Resources:
FreeTranslation.com
   <http://www.freetranslation.com/>
Babelfish Text Translator
   <http://babelfish.altavista.com>

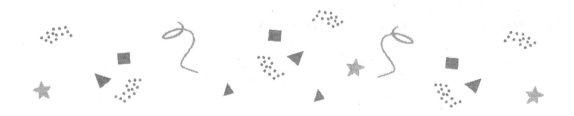

Celebrate National Handwriting Day

Subject: Penmanship, Social Studies
Grade level: 3 to 5

Celebrate January 12, the birthday of John Hancock, by improving the penmanship of your name.

Activity Title:
Sign Here

Materials:

Student journals, pens (regular or calligraphy) or pencils, word processing software

Procedure:

John Hancock was very proud of his excellent penmanship. Have the students examine his signature on a paper copy of the Declaration of Independence or by using the primary sources on the Web. Explain the defiant nature of signing this document and the penalties of treason.

Have the students practice their signature in their journals using a variety of pens or pencils. Use a word processing application and different fonts for them to type their name, print it, and keep it for their journal.

If a computer writing tablet is available, let students try to write their signature digitally. Save the signature as a bitmap to be used on their classroom computer assignments.

Evaluation:

Students will learn about John Hancock's defiant signing of the Declaration of Independence and will practice writing their signature.

Resources:

Koslow, Philip. *John Hancock: A Signature Life*. New York: Franklin Watts, 1998.
Fritz, Jean. *Will You Sign Here, John Hancock?* New York: PaperStar Books, 1997.
The Declaration of Independence
    <http://www.nara.gov/exhall/charters/declaration/decmain.html>

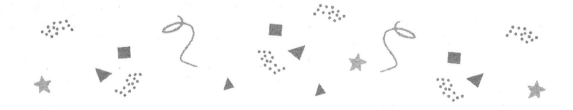

Celebrate Martin L. King Jr.'s Birthday

Subject: Social Studies, Language Arts

Grade level: K to 5

Celebrate Dr. King's Birthday on January 15 by learning about his life and work in civil rights.

Activity Title:
Freedom Dreaming

Materials:
Web site access, books on the topic

Procedure:
Create a classroom display about Dr. Martin L. King. Have the students add to this display by reading about Dr. King's life and work for peace.

Older students can reflect on King's famous speech and what its message means to them.

Evaluation:
Students will learn about civil rights and the Nobel Peace Prize

Resources:
Dr. Martin L. King Scavenger Hunt
    <http://users.massed.net/~tstrong/Martin.htm>
A Teeny Tiny Book About Martin L. King
    <http://www.bry-backmanor.org/mlk.html>
The Nobel Peace Prize
    <http://www.nobel.se/peace/articles/lundestad/>

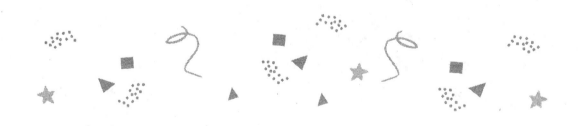

Celebrate Benjamin Franklin's Birthday

Subject: Social Studies, Language Arts
Grade level: 5

Celebrate Ben Franklin's Birthday on January 17 by learning about the busy life of this inventor and statesman.

Activity Title:
Electric Ideas

Materials:

Biographies of Ben Franklin, Web site access

Procedure:

Make a class list of the many inventions of Ben Franklin. If you read Jean Fritz's book, find out what the Big Idea was. What rules for "good behavior" do you think have value today?

Analyze the meaning of some of his proverbs, such as "Eat to live and not live to eat." Did he follow his own advice?

Evaluation:

Students will learn about invention, rules for living, and proverbs.

Resources:

Aliki. *The Many Lives of Benjamin Franklin*. Englewood: Prentice Hall, Inc., 1997.
Fritz, Jean. *What's the Big Idea, Ben Franklin?* New York: Coward-McCann, Inc., 1976.
Poor Richard's Almanack
        <http://sln.fi.edu/qa98/musing9/almanack1733.html>
Quotes by Benjamin Franklin
        <http://www.ushistory.org/franklin/fun/index.htm>

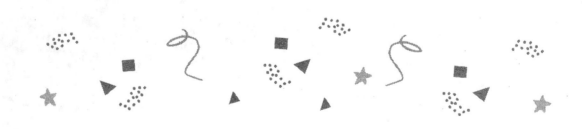

Celebrate Pooh Day

Subject: Reading

Grade level: K to 2

Celebrate the Birthday of A.A. Milne on January 18 by reading some of his works.

Activity Title:
Pooh and Beyond

Materials:

Books by A. A. Milne, student journals

Procedure:

Younger students can celebrate this day with a birthday party for Winnie the Pooh. Older students can read the poem "Disobedience" from Milne's book *When We Were Very Young*. (This poem is a favorite of the Frazel family.)

Have the students reflect on being disobedient and taking responsibility for their actions in their journals.

Evaluation:

Students will enjoy stories and poems written by this favorite children's author.

Resources:

Milne, A.A. *When We Were Very Young*. New York: Puffin Books, 1976.
The Page at Pooh Corner
    <http://www.electrontrap.org/jmilne/Pooh/>

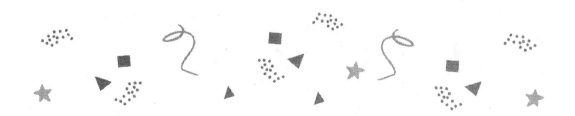

Celebrate National Soup Month

Subject: Reading

Grade level: K to 3

> Evaluation: Students will enjoy stories and poems written by this favorite children's author.

Activity Title:

Soup Kettle

Materials:

Copy of one of the versions of "Stone Soup"

Procedure:

There are many versions of this classic folktale about trickery and deception. This is a must read aloud to the class for National Soup Month. Of course, soup should be served for lunch.

Have students list their favorite soups and bring in any family soup recipes from home to share with the class.

Evaluation:

Students will learn about a classic folktale and enjoy soup on a cold January day.

Resources:

Brown, Marcia. *Stone Soup*. New York: Aladdin Books, 1986.
TeacherView: Stone Soup
      <http://www.eduplace.com/tview/pages/s/Stone_Soup_Marcia_Brown.html>

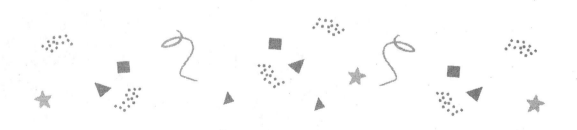

Celebrate Everyone's Birthday

Subject: Interdisciplinary

Grade level: K to 5

> Robert Louis Stevenson wrote that children whose birthday fell on a holiday or special event are disappointed not to have their own special day. He suggested those children celebrate their birthday on his birthday as a substitute. Set aside a day during the second week of January for a classroom birthday celebration, because the most often celebrated event in our lives is our birthday.

Activity Title:
Famous Birthdays

Materials:

Web site access, student journals, library visit

Procedure:

Use the suggested Web site to have students find a famous person who shares their birthday. Have the student write about that person in their journal after researching them at the school library. Students can then write their own autobiography in their student journals.

Students can create a list of the birthdates of all the students in the class. As a math activity, have the students figure out who is the oldest or youngest student in the class, or calculate how many days old they are now and on their next birthday.

Celebrate everybody's birthday by having a class party.

Evaluation:

Students will use a birthday theme to perform "birthday math" and research a famous person born on their own birthday

Resources:

Famous Birthdays
   <http://www.famousbirthdays.com/bdayhome.html>
Connecting Students: Biography
   <http://www.connectingstudents.com/themes/bios.htm>

Celebrate Learning About Medieval Times

Subject: Social Studies, Art
Grade level: 4 to 5

Celebrate learning about the Middle Ages by learning about heraldry. In the Middle Ages, knights decorated their shields so others could identify them while they were wearing armor. These designs resulted in family coats of arms with mottos describing their point of view.

Activity Title:

Design a Shield

Materials:

Reproducible Activity 88: Design a Shield, student journals, art supplies, Web site access

Procedure:

Photocopy enough copies of Reproducible Activity 88: Design a Shield for each student to have one. Have students choose a shape for their shield, trace it into their journals, and decorate it.

Have students think up their own motto (blazon) and write about it in their journals.

Evaluation:

Student will design a shield and learn about mottos with this hands-on activity.

Resources:

Nicolle, David. Medieval Knights. New York: Viking, 1997.
Gander Academy's Introduction to Heraldry
    <http://www.stemnet.nf.ca/CITE/medieval_heraldry_into.htm>

Activity 88: Design a Shield

Name _____

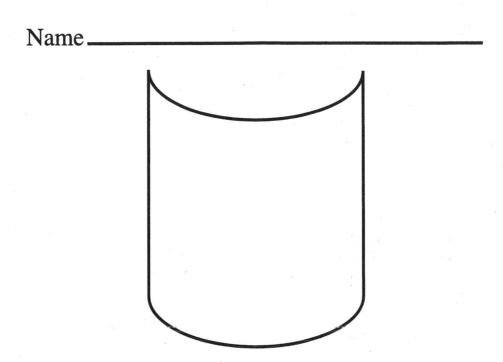

Name _____

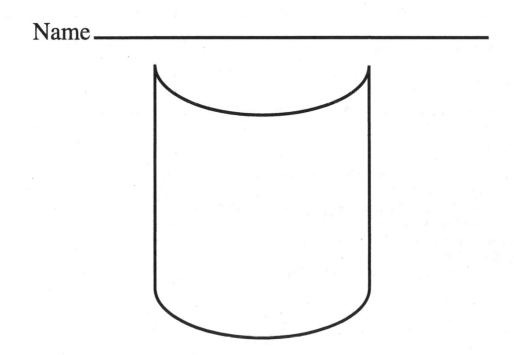

Celebrate Learning About Owls

Subject: Science

Grade level: 3 to 5

> January is a great time to celebrate learning about animal biology and habitats. This activity is about owls but could be adapted to another animal of your choice.

Activity Title:
Wise Owls

Materials:

Encyclopedias (traditional print, CD-ROM, or Web-based), library visit, art materials, whiteboard, Reproducible Activity 21: KWL Graphic Organizer

Procedure:

Divide the students into groups and explain the classroom rules for group projects. Plan time each day for group meetings and group report preparation.

Use this month-long classroom project to teach skills in science and research. Use Reproducible Activity 21: KWL Graphic Organizer to help students narrow the topics to be researched.

Assign some of the work as homework, but provide class time for students to work as a cooperative unit.

Design a rubric for the student presentations or for the classroom learning center displays.

Evaluation:

Students will participate in a group project revolving around the theme of animal study.

Resources:

Yolen, Jane. *Owl Moon*. New York: Philomel Books, 1987.
Connecting Students: Owl Moon
    <http://www.connectingstudents.com/literacy/owl_moon.htm>
Gander Academy's Owl Resources
    <http://www.stemnet.nf.ca/CITE/owls.htm>
ABC Teach: Owl Theme
    <http://www.abcteach.com/Owls/OwlTOC.htm>

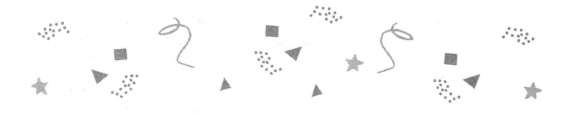

Celebrate National Book Month

Subject: Reading

Grade level: 3 to 5

Celebrate National Book Month by learning about the Newbery and Caldecott book awards.

Activity Title:
Book Awards

Materials:
Web site access, books that have won the Newbery or Caldecott award

Procedure:
Use the Web to visit the Newbery and Caldecott Award Web page to learn about the awards, who the awards were named for, and to get a list of the award-winning books.

Visit the school library media center or public library to have the students choose a book to read from the lists.

Use the suggested Web sites to connect the resources of the Web to the books.

Evaluation:
Students will learn about the awards for excellence in children's books.

Resources:
Award Web pages at the ALA
    <http://www.ala.org/alsc/newbery.html>
    <http://www.ala.org/alsc/caldecott.html>
Newberys & the Net: Thematic Technology Connections
    <http://www.eduscapes.com/newbery/new.html>
Connecting Students: Caldecott Medal Resources
    <http://www.connectingstudents.com/themes/caldecott.htm>

Celebrate Learning About Japan

Subject: Interdisciplinary
Grade level: K to 5

Celebrate learning about the country of Japan with an activity on paper folding.

Activity Title:
Origami

Materials:

Origami paper, markers

Procedure:

On the classroom map, point out the location of Japan. Use books from the school library media center for learning about this country. You can team the students for this project. You also can use the suggested Web sites designed for students. Studying or writing Haiku poetry also is a great activity when studying Japan.

Use the Zoom School to locate directions for the art of origami. Print out these directions, read them with the students, create the art, and display the decorations.

Evaluation:

Students will learn about Japan's art and poetry.

Resources:

Zoom School: Japan
    <http://www.enchantedlearning.com/school/Japan/>
Zoom School Japanese Crafts
    <http://www.enchantedlearning.com/crafts/japan/>
Kids Japan
    <http://www.kids-japan.com/>

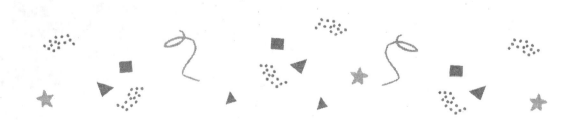

Celebrate Learning About Money

Subject: Math

Grade level: 3 to 5

Celebrate money this month by beginning a math unit about currency.

Activity Title:

Famous Faces on Money

Materials:

Web site access

Procedure:

Make arrangements for a class field trip to a local bank. Ask the bank to have some paper and coin money for the students to examine. Have your students identify whose face appears on which bill, and which famous buildings also appear.

Discuss counterfeiting issues with the students. Emphasize that it is illegal to create your own money on the computer.

Evaluation:

Students will begin a math unit on money with an authentic experience.

Resources:

United States Treasury Kid's Page
    <http://www.ustreas.gov/kids/>
Who's on the Money?
    <http://www.ustreas.gov/currency/>
US Secret Service: Know Your Money
    <http://www.treas.gov/usss/money_detect.htm>

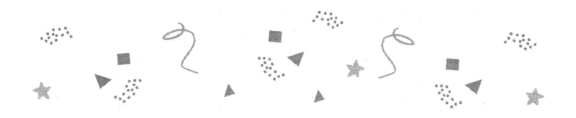

Celebrate Inauguration Day

Subject: Social Studies

Grade level: 5

> Inauguration Day is the day when the President-elect and Vice President-elect take the oath of office. This is a ceremony that takes place on January 20 after the Presidential elections in November.

Activity Title:

The Presidency

Materials:

Encyclopedias (traditional print, CD-ROM, or Web-based), Web site access

Procedure:

Because this day is not celebrated each year, have your students take this day to learn about past ceremonies or learn about the life of a President of their choice. You can even have them take an online quiz!

Evaluation:

Students will learn what happens on this day and learn some new facts about the new or current President.

Resources:

Inauguration Day
    <http://www.pbs.org/newshour/inauguration/inauguration_day.html>
Inaugural Quiz
    <http://www.nara.gov/nara/digital/quiz/quiz.html>
42Explore Topic: Presidents of the United States
    <http://eduscapes.com/42explore/presidt.htm>

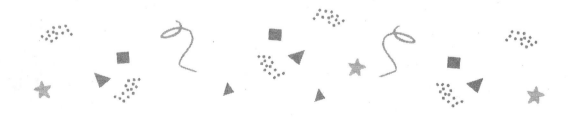

Celebrate Mozart's Birthday

Subject: Music

Grade level: 3 to 5

Celebrate Mozart's birthday on January 27 (1756) with a study of the orchestra.

Activity Title:
Kids Listen

Materials:
Music teacher, tapes or audio CDs of Mozart's music, musical instruments provided by the music teacher

Procedure:
With the cooperation of the music teacher, learn about the orchestra, classical music, and musical instruments.

Have students investigate the life of Mozart and listen to some of his compositions.

Evaluation:
Students will learn about the orchestra to celebrate Mozart's birthday.

Resources:
Brighton, Catherine. *Mozart: Scenes from the Childhood of the Great Composer*. New York: Doubleday, 1990.
Listen up! Turning Up!
    <http://www.pbs.org/wgbh/pops/listenup/index.html>
Composers: Mozart
    <http://www.essentialsofmusic.com/composer/mozart.html>
42Explore Topic: Musical Instruments
    <http://eduscapes.com/42explore/musicmnts.htm>

Celebrate Chinese New Year

Subject: Interdisciplinary

Grade level: 2 to 5

> The Chinese New Year doesn't coincide with our own on January 1, but many Chinese-Americans celebrate it in the winter.

Activity Title:
What Year Is It?

Materials:
Books on the topic, Web site access

Procedure:
The Chinese New Year will be celebrated on 2/1/2003, 1/22/2004, 2/9/2005, and 1/29/2006 (Source: Calendars Through the Ages: The Chinese Calendar), so bridge the months of January and February with this multicultural event in your classroom. Visit the listed Web sites for special information and activities.

Evaluation:
Students will learn about a different New Year's celebration and its relationship to our calendar.

Resources:
Hoyt-Goldsmith, Diane. *Celebrating Chinese New Year*. New York: Holiday House, 1998
Schaefer, Lola M. *Chinese New Year*. Mankato, MN: Pebble Books/Capstone Press, 2001.
Chinese New Year
    <http://www.educ.uvic.ca/faculty/mroth/438/CHINA/chinese_new_year.html>
Calendars Through the Ages: The Chinese Calendar
    <http://webexhibits.org/calendars/calendar-chinese.html>
Lucky Red Envelopes Activity
    <http://www.newton.mec.edu/Angier/DimSum/china__dim_sum_red_envelop.html>
Accordian Dragon Activity
    <http://www.newton.mec.edu/Angier/DimSum/Accordian%20Dragon%20Lesson.html>
Kids Domain: Chinese New Year
    <http://www.kidsdomain.com/holiday/chineseny.html>

Celebrate National Puzzle Day

Subject: Math

Grade level: 3 to 5

Have an "a-maze-ing" day by celebrating National Puzzle Day (January 29) by solving printed mazes.

Activity Title:
Inside the Maze

Materials:
Web site access, books with mazes

Procedure:
Copy or print out (from the Web) a variety of mazes for students to solve.

Evaluation:
Students will develop higher order visual perception skills by solving puzzles in the form of mazes.

Resources:
Discovery School's PuzzleMaker
     <http://puzzlemaker.school.discovery.com/index.html>

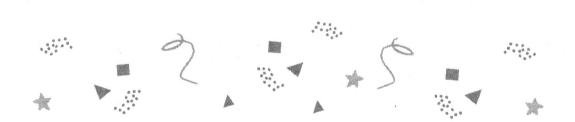

Celebrate Jackie Robinson's Birthday

Subject: Language Arts

Grade level: 4 to 5

Jackie Robinson was born on January 31, 1919, and was the first African-American baseball player to play major league baseball. Celebrate his birthday with a team project.

Activity Title:

First to Play

Materials:

Biographical material on Jackie Robinson, Web site access

Procedure:

Have a team of students research the life of Jackie Robinson and prepare an informal presentation to celebrate his birthday. Students can volunteer to work on this project to increase student enthusiasm for teamwork.

Evaluation:

Students will learn about the life and point of view from a man who was not only a great sports hero but also a civil rights advocate.

Resources:

Beyond the Playing Field
   <http://www.nara.gov/education/teaching/robinson/robmain.html>
Jackie Robinson
   <http://www.afroam.org/history/Robinson/intro.html>

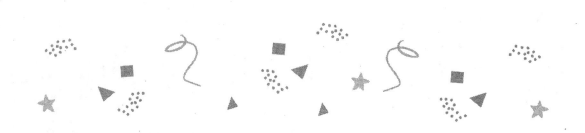

Bibliography

Print Resources

Chase's Calendar of Events. 2001 ed. Chicago: Contemporary Books, 2001.

Cohen, Hennig, and Tristram Potter Coffin, eds. *The Folklore of American Holidays*. 3rd ed. Detroit: Gale Group, 1999.

Dunkling, Leslie. *A Dictionary of Days*. New York: Facts on File Publications, 1988.

Haglund, Elaine J., and Marcia L. Harris. *On This Day: A Collection of Everyday Learning Events and Activities for the Media Center, Library and Classroom*. Littleton: Libraries Unlimited, Inc., 1983.

Henderson, Helene, and Ellen Thompson, eds. *Holidays, Festivals and Celebrations of the World*. Detroit: Omnigraphics, Inc., 1997.

Macmillan Profiles: Festivals and Holidays. New York: Macmillan Library Reference USA, 1999.

Simpson, Carol. *Daily Journals*. Parsippany, NJ: Good Year Books, 1993.

Web Sites

Classroom Connect's Connected Teacher Calendar. 15 Sept. 2001 <http://www1.classroom.com/community/connection/calendar.jhtml>.

History Channel's This Day in History. 15 Sept. 2001 <http://www.historychannel.com/thisday/>.

The Holiday Zone. 15 Sept. 2001 <http://www.theholidayzone.com/>.

Infoplease.com Daily Almanac. 15 Sept. 2001 <http://ln.infoplease.com/cgi-bin/daily>.

NOBLE (North of Boston Library Exchange) Web: Through the Year. 15 Sept. 2001 <http://www.noblenet.org/year/>.

Wilstar's Holiday Page. 15 Sept. 2001 <http://wilstar.com/holidays/>.

Worldwide Holiday and Festival Site. 15 Sept. 2001 <http://www.holidayfestival.com/>.

Yahoo: Holidays and Observances. 15 Sept. 2001 <http://dir.yahoo.com/Society_and_Culture/holidays_and_observances/>.

Yahooligan's This Day in History. 15 Sept. 2001 <http://www.yahooligans.com/docs/tdih/>.

❖ Index ❖